A collective vision of pastors, members, and administrators to multiply the kingdom of God in North America through baptizing, equipping, and planting.

JOSÉ H. CORTES JR. AND IVAN L. WILLIAMS SR. EDITORS

Pacific Press®
Publishing Association

Nampa, Idaho | www.pacificpress.com

Cover design by Gerald Lee Monks
Cover design resources from iStockphoto.com | rikkyal
Inside design by Aaron Troia

Copyright © 2020 by Pacific Press® Publishing Association
Printed in the United States of America
All rights reserved

The authors assume full responsibility for the accuracy of all facts and quotations as cited in this book.

Additional copies of this book may be purchased by calling toll-free 1-800-765-6955 or by visiting AdventistBookCenter.com.

Library of Congress Cataloging-in-Publication Data
Names: Cortes, Jose H., 1949- editor. | Williams, Ivan L., editor.
Title: Multiply / edited by Jose Cortes, Jr. and Ivan Williams.
Description: Nampa, Idaho : Pacific Press Publishing Association, 2020. |
    Summary: "An evangelism and church growth manual for pastors"-- Provided by publisher.
Identifiers: LCCN 2020030698 (print) | LCCN 2020030699 (ebook) |
    ISBN 9780816366729 (paperback) | ISBN 9780816366736 (kindle edition)
Subjects: LCSH: Church growth. | Evangelistic work. | Pastoral theology.
Classification: LCC BV652.25 .M85 2020 (print) | LCC BV652.25 (ebook) |
    DDC 254/.5--dc23
LC record available at https://lccn.loc.gov/2020030698
LC ebook record available at https://lccn.loc.gov/2020030699

November 2020

Contents

FOREWORD

Is It Worth Sharing?

How does the gospel transform the opioid addict, the affluent, skeptical urbanite, the judgmental self-righteous, the divorced, single parent, or the person stuck in a cycle of failure due to their own choices? Before you put this book down to collect dust or pass it off as another book on evangelism, I challenge you to take another look.

Even though soul-winning and discipleship are increasing in the North American Division, however slowly, future growth is vitally dependent upon the urgent need for greater community connectedness, proclamation, compassion, revitalization, and church planting. This urgent need serves as the heart of this book. The need also forges a working definition for evangelism in our division as "Reach, Retain, and Reclaim the people of North America with Jesus' mission and message of compassion, hope, and wholeness."

The essence of the gospel is to "multiply." It was set in motion by Jesus when He told His followers to "go therefore and make disciples of all nations, baptizing them in the name of the Father and of the Son and the Holy Spirit" (Matthew 28:19, RSV). This multiplication charge is the lifeblood of the gospel, and the church is fueled forward through this "sending" or "going." Even though Jesus did not marry us to a particular method or solidify specific means or ways of reaching people, He did model it with His life and ministry. He sent out followers two by two and taught them how to love, teach, be present, care, meet needs, and live, which is the essence of discipleship.

The gospel was never meant to be exclusive or confined to Christians only. It does not belong to an "in crowd" or "out crowd." Christ's instructions included sharing with the entire world—every race, language, tongue, and people. The mission to touch and tell the world consists of connecting with everyday people, churched and unchurched—those who choose faith and those who question faith, those who doubt spiritual authority and those who are skeptical of religion.

Isolating the good news to oneself is not an option, because it leads to the same failed missional results of those who lived before us, as expressed by Dragutin Matak in his article, "The Misuse of History Through Religious Exclusiveness as a Major Obstacle to the Transmission of the Gospel." He wrote, "The ancient Jews could not fully achieve their mission to the world because they claimed their rich history for themselves, instead of sharing it and appreciating that their Benefactor was ready to bestow wonderful blessings on them and all the earth. They mummified Abraham, Isaac, Jacob, and Moses in their history instead of sharing the spirituality of the patriarchs with the whole world."[1]

Are we as Seventh-day Adventists repeating history? An exclusive faith is contrary to an inclusive Father who sent His Son to die for everyone. Broken people, scarred by failed trust, past abuse, loneliness, and suffering, are looking for places to be accepted, places to exhale, places to be fulfilled, on the journey of life. The everlasting gospel of a crucified, risen, soon-coming Lord announced by the three angels (Revelation 14:6–12) is our only hope for this dying world. Jesus is the only One who can bear the load, the guilt, the shame, the failure, and the pain of living a life without constraint. What Jesus has done should compel us to spread the good news.

With this passion, our division, union, and conference evangelism leaders have created a missional guide expressing six outcomes or action steps to reach, reclaim, and retain the people of North America with Jesus' mission and message of compassion, hope, and wholeness. These action steps are intuitive, incarnational, and relational:

> **Action 1—Love:** Multiply through fostering connection points that are welcoming and safe.
> **Action 2—Serve:** Multiply through engaging all members in ministry and mission.
> **Action 3—Baptize:** Multiply through providing many opportunities for people to commit to Jesus and the church.
> **Action 4—Equip:** Multiply through mentoring members who make disciples.
> **Action 5—Plant:** Multiply through community-based church planting.
> **Action 6—Revitalize:** Multiply through diagnosing and implementing growth strategies for plateaued and declining churches.

Our world is in desperate need of a gospel message it can hear and see, one that transforms both the hearer and the messenger, and one that includes all broken humanity. Long gone are the days of being impersonal, irrelevant, and uninformed about the questions people are asking. Studying the longings and interests of the human heart is essential in reaching it.

Finally, if the message we profess does not make us like Jesus, it will be viewed as phony and lose its attractiveness no matter how true it may be. "No one has ever been reclaimed from a wrong position by censure and reproach, but many have thus been driven from Christ and led to seal their hearts against conviction." On the other hand, "the revelation of Christ in your own character will have a transforming power upon all with whom you come in contact."[2]

I am excited about this book! In it, the authors give accounts of dynamic experiences that provide keys to help you multiply the kingdom. As you read, you will find evangelistic encouragement, practical tools, and useful approaches to reach your community with the gospel worth sharing!

Ivan L. Williams Sr.
director, NAD Ministerial Association

---

1. Dragutin Matak, "The Misuse of History Through Religious Exclusiveness as a Major Obstacle to the Transmission of the Gospel," *Biblijski pogledi* 21, nos. 1, 2 (2013): 349, https://hrcak.srce.hr/index.php?show=clanak&id_clanak_jezik=207548.

2. Ellen G. White, *Thoughts From the Mount of Blessing* (Mountain View, CA: Pacific Press®, 1956), 129.

ACTION 1—LOVE

Multiply through fostering
connection points that are
welcoming and safe.

Parents and Pastors, Please Make Room!

Jose Cortes Jr.

But Jesus said, "Let the children come to me. Don't stop them! For the
Kingdom of Heaven belongs to those who are like these children."
                                                    —Matthew 19:14, NLT

A few years ago, as sixteen students of South Lancaster Academy, who had requested baptism during that week of prayer, were about to be baptized at the fully packed Village Adventist Church in South Lancaster, Massachusetts, something unimaginable happened. Our then six-year-old son Joel managed to get away from my wife, Joanne, and run toward the platform. He began to climb, trying to get into the baptistry.

As everyone looked on, I asked him, "Joel, what are you doing?" He replied: "I want to get baptized; I've been asking you for three years. You are already in the water, let me get in and baptize me. Please, Papa, I love Jesus, just do it!" Rather than being excited and moved by my little boy's act of faith and boldness, I was angered by his "irreverence" and mortified by the "distraction" he had just created in the midst of such a sacred ceremony. I tried to convince him to no avail to go back and sit next to his mom. As he continued to make his case softly and bravely to me, before hundreds of people who watched in awe, I stared at him in disapproval as I waited for Joanne to come and retrieve him. It felt like she took forever to get there. When she finally got there, she brought him down, gave him her phone, and asked him to take a photo of the baptism. After fussing and telling her that he was there to be baptized and not to take photos, he ended up taking a few pictures.

Evangelism Action 1—Love
Multiply through fostering connection points that are welcoming and safe.

As I think of this very personal and painful story, I am reminded of our first evangelism action. From 2015 to 2020, we surveyed and discussed evangelism with thousands of pastors, members, and church leaders. Our study resulted in six actions that could revolutionize mission and evangelism across North America. Eighty-seven percent ranked "love" at 7 or higher on a 1–10 scale. The point of this action is to make it easy to come in and very hard to get out. I am not talking about a prison system here; rather, I am referring to a type of church that is accessible, welcoming, loving, and empowering to such a degree that once you come in, you want to stay and do life together with this awesome community of believers.

If you do not have people from all walks of life in your church, perhaps it is because they feel your church is not a safe place for them. Is your baptism process long and complicated? Does your congregation understand baptism to be the graduation, only for those who have all the knowledge and have shown great spiritual maturity, rather than a new birth and a beginning step in the discipleship journey? If so, your church perhaps is not accessible. Remember that in the New Testament, baptism was always the step that followed the acceptance of Jesus as Lord and Savior, and it was to be continued by a beautiful discipleship journey of fellowship, breaking bread together, teaching, confirmation, service, and engagement in the faith.

If your church is not intentionally allowing children to be baptized as they accept Jesus, and if the phrases "too young" and "not ready yet" are common responses to their requests for baptism, perhaps your church is not very accessible. Keep in mind that there are no age requirements for baptism in Scripture. According to the Bible, baptism is not for the perfect; it is not for those who know all the doctrines (although knowing our beliefs is important). Baptism is for sinners who have accepted Jesus as their Lord and Savior.

Members must be empowered to treat people who are different from us the way Jesus would. Additionally, ensure that your church is accepting, accessible, and safe. To do this, establish serious guidelines for children's safety. Create clear, quality signage that identifies your church positively around the community. Furthermore, provide an updated website and an active social media presence.

As I look back to my initial story, I still regret my reaction! If that happened today, I would allow Joel to climb over into the baptistry and would baptize him on the spot. On that day I learned a few lessons, first as a father but also as a pastor: (1) There is no minimum age requirement to accept Jesus. (2) The decision of a child to follow Jesus needs to be celebrated and taken seriously. (3) My children and all children are more important than what people may think or say. (4) The salvation of my children and all children is more valuable than some long-held views (traditions) that state an individual must be a "certain age" before he or she gets baptized (I am not referring to infant baptism here). (5) Children are people, and Jesus is still available to them at the time of their choosing. Finally, (6) as a pastor, I am not here to hinder a decision to follow Jesus, but to facilitate it.

Needless to say, Joel was baptized three weeks later at the age of six, together with his brother Jose, who was seven, and Ralph, a friend who participated with them in the small-group Bible study for children we held weekly at our home. On several occasions, Joel, who is now older, has told me that his baptism is the number one highlight of his life!

Dear parent or pastor, please learn from my mistake! Do not delay a child's decision to follow Jesus because he or she is too young! Or for any other reason!

Please, take the time to talk with your congregation about the most practical ways to make your church accepting of people and the most accessible and spiritually safe experience in your community.

Chapter 1

Love People Into Your Church

David B. Franklin

Bruce was missing for several weeks. Given the volatile nature of living on the streets of Baltimore, we were concerned but prayed for the best. After we had searched for him for a few months, one Saturday morning, Bruce returned to our hot-meal program. However, this time he was not looking to receive a meal; he had a story to tell. To our delight, Bruce had not become a victim of the harsh realities of homelessness in Baltimore. He was working hard to pull the pieces of his life together. In just a few short months, Bruce had managed to find a job and secure transitional housing. He was preparing to move into his own apartment a few days after we reconnected. It was such a joy to see such a quick transition. He was excited about his future and motivated to keep reaching for his goals.

Bruce, however, was not satisfied with his progress. He said, "It's not enough for me to succeed; I want everyone down here to succeed." He continued, "Pastor, they appreciate you, but they really listen to me." That day, Bruce did not return for food; he returned for friendship. He was committed to his friends and wanted to do everything in his power to help them experience the progress he experienced.

Bruce exemplified the message Jesus shares in the parable of the lost sheep (Matthew 18:12–14; Luke 15:3–7). In the parable, Jesus illustrates the value of an individual. The shepherd leaves the fold to search for one sheep who is lost. In a similar manner, Bruce left the comforts of his new life to find his friends and show them how to experience a new reality. He was willing to make sacrifices, forgo comfort, and spend time reaching his friends. We learned several lessons from Bruce that day. However, the most important was that real relationships require active responsibility. This simple lesson has shaped the way we do ministry at Miracle City Church.

100K Touches campaign

In 2016, Miracle City Church embarked on a campaign called 100K Touches. We committed to reaching our community with 100,000 acts of service within a year. We divided our projects into six categories: homelessness, education, food, insecurity, economic development, and temporary crisis. Beginning in January, we invited members to serve. They could either sign up to serve for projects throughout the week or join us on Saturday mornings for our Big Serve Days. On Big Serve Days, members gathered at eight o'clock in the morning for a simple breakfast and a brief time of prayer and worship. Afterward, project teams huddled together for instructions and then deployed to locations all over the city. Some packed food for sick patients, others entered laundromats to surprise patrons with free loads of laundry, others visited local schools to refresh libraries and hallways, and still others participated in our hot meals for the homeless program.

During this year, through partnership with local nonprofit organizations and the creativity of members in our congregation, we hosted job fairs, painted schools, cleaned up parks, launched an after-school program, provided fresh produce from Whole Foods to residents, supported literacy programs, started a community garden, visited nursing homes, and so much more. As a result, by the grace of God, we completed 127,569 touches, exceeding our goal in only eight months.

The importance of this initiative for our congregation is hard to overstate. Our congregation began to view church less as an event and more as a community. We began to see our worship experience as a place to share stories of victory, pray with one another, and "refuel" to go out and serve others. We also learned that making a sustainable impact would require a different approach. In many ways, Bruce had shared all we needed to know, but it took some time to unpack the lessons his example provided. However, after several conversations and some sincere prayer, we discovered a better way forward. The rest of this section will be devoted to sharing some principles we learned on how to engage effectively in community outreach through developing loving relationships.

Relationships

All effective community outreach begins with relationships built upon mutual love and respect. The word *mutual* is important. Relationships are meant to be a two-way street, to maintain a balance of give-and-take that is fueled by mutual responsibility. As a church family, Miracle City did not always take this approach to community outreach; however, Bruce showed us a better way.

Bruce returned to the hot-meal program to find his friends because of the relationships he had established with them. His friends were there with him during tough times, and now he felt a responsibility to help them during their rough times. He loved his friends, and they loved him as well. Their mutual love gave Bruce the unique ability to reach them in ways that we could not. In fact, their mutuality was the key ingredient that allowed Bruce's friends to listen, learn, and, ultimately, change. One of the greatest barriers to effective community outreach is that we fail to develop relationships built upon mutuality.

Let us return for a moment to the parable of the lost sheep. If we consider our place in that story, we must acknowledge we have all been the lost sheep. However, sometimes in our genuine effort to follow the example of the Chief Shepherd, we can forget that we are all sheep. This thinking can inadvertently produce a superior-inferior relational construct between the church members and the community members. When this happens, church members often see community members as a project and not as partners. In addition, community members could see church members as manipulative, invaders, or, even worse, destructive. All of this works against effective ministry to those in our communities.

If we are going to minister to our communities effectively, we must build relationships full of mutual love and respect. It will require us to accept that we not only have something to give but also have much we need to receive. Churches must learn to listen to community members in order to understand not only their needs but also their strengths. Every community has strengths that can be empowered to assist community members in identifying solutions to the challenges that exist in their community. However, churches never learn of these strengths without entering into balanced relationships in which both the church and the community see that they have something to give and something to receive. When we have relationships built upon our mutuality, we open the door to engaging effectively in community outreach in a way that grows our churches and strengthens the community at the same time. Maybe even more important, our church members will begin to see that baptism and community building all qualify as kingdom building.

It is important to build relationships with various groups in our communities:

- Residents
- Students
- Community association members and leaders
- School principals
- Community center directors and staff
- After-school program directors
- Local business owners
- City council members

Reputation

Initially, the 100K Touches campaign helped our church develop a good reputation in the community. However, it fell short of building deep relationships with the community members, primarily because we unintentionally structured our outreach for people to receive assistance but not to build relationships.

So was all of the effort wasted? Not at all. During the 100K Touches campaign, we realized we had stumbled upon a formula for building relationships within communities. When a church is unknown to the surrounding neighborhood, it must build a reputation that allows the community to begin trusting the church. Service projects that meet temporary needs are one way to build the reputation of the church, which in turn opens the door to establishing relationships with community members. However, members of the church must be keenly aware that the goal of the service project is not to give out the most sandwiches, blankets, coats, or other items. The goal is to create space for relationships to grow. Members of the congregation must give attention to more than packing bags and filling baskets. Instead, members must take a genuine interest in the lives of those who are coming to receive assistance. Service projects are just one way to build the reputation of the church. Other programs could provide the same level of interest or visibility. The goal is to create space for church members and community members to connect.

To assist our church members with understanding this principle of outreach, we adopted a term as our guiding philosophy—*disinterested benevolence*. In our use of the term, *disinterested benevolence* simply means to do good for the sake of doing good without expecting anything in return. We rehearsed this term and its meaning at every outreach meeting. Before every Big Serve Day, we posted it on the Serve page of our website and shared it during our worship experiences. We wanted to prioritize the people over the projects and ensure that members of the community did not feel that our outreach was just a tool to rope them into attending a Bible study or church service. We knew that to build trust, there must be no strings attached so that genuine love could drive all of our trust-building work.

Revitalization

Once trust has been established and church members and leaders have relationships with community members and leaders, the next phase of outreach can begin—community revitalization. Community revitalization focuses on rebuilding the broken systems within communities. The relationships we built in our community brought us face-to-face with residents living in homes with toxic amounts of mold growth, families without access to quality food, educational institutions struggling to make a budget, and a host of economic issues that make it nearly impossible to escape poverty. We found it difficult to say we love people and then give no attention to the troubles they face every day as they attempt to access the necessities of life. Our love for community members guided us to explore how we could collectively revitalize the broken institutions in our community and remove some of the real barriers to receiving the gospel.

Here is the amazing thing about relationships: they are unpredictable and often take us places we would never expect. When we started the 100K Touches campaign, we never imagined that the relationships we established would lay the groundwork for our congregation to become a leader in revitalizing our community. We did not plan to be involved in (nor did we understand) community revitalization, but our relationships guided us to see where real change was possible. Even more important, our relationships inspired us because we now understand that this work will impact not only the residents of our community today but the residents of our community for many generations to come.

Community revitalization should not be mistaken for community outreach. At Miracle City Church, we view them as two different types of engagement. Community outreach focuses on building a reputation that leads to developing relationships. Community revitalization focuses on collaboratively working to strengthen community systems that are failing the community. For us, this means we have two teams with different focuses. One team focuses on community outreach projects, and the other focuses on community revitalization initiatives that cover education, housing, economic development, and health and wellness. We firmly believe that following the example of Jesus means creating healthy communities for people to live and dwell in.

It is important to note that community revitalization is not a quick fix for growing a church. It is not about tallying up enough work so we can predetermine the number of people who will accept Jesus. At Miracle City Church, we accept that we will not easily be able to determine when community members may take the next step toward accepting Jesus. However, we believe that making the love of Jesus visible through community revitalization will bear fruit in due season.

Bruce's example helps to expand on this idea. Bruce could not determine if, or when, his friends would take advantage of the information he had to offer. However, he continued to stay in those relationships even when some chose not to follow through on his advice. There was no magic moment when Bruce determined he had done enough. He committed to the responsibility of maintaining relationships and sharing his life with his friends.

When we started the 100K Touches campaign, we simply sought to do good for our community. However, after we completed the 100K Touches campaign, we moved on to complete several projects that helped us begin the work of community revitalization by expanding our ability to build relationships. We hosted a Community Baby Shower, a Back-to-School Block Party, a Community Baby Blessing, and a fellowship event called Christmas Around the World. We also adopted the local elementary schools in our neighborhood. We renovated the school library, updated a faculty resource lounge, replaced the flooring in the main auditorium, repainted hallways, refreshed an administrative office, and opened an after-school program focused on reading and technology.

After a major flood event in our community, we raised money to renovate twenty-three homes. We replaced water heaters and furnaces and updated basements to prevent water from returning into those homes. Each of these projects has given us an opportunity to build relationships with residents, school principals, community association presidents, community center directors, local business owners, and city council members. Now, as plans are being discussed to revitalize the community, the church is a leading voice in those discussions.

Here are some questions to consider when preparing for community revitalization:

- What organizations (such as schools, nonprofits organizations,

businesses) are located in the community that can become potential partners in the work of revitalization?
- What strengths and assets exist in the community that could better serve the needs of the community if they had additional support (human and/or financial)?
- What strengths and assets exist within the church that can support areas of need in the community?
- What has the church learned from its relationships in the community, and how can that inform the way the church chooses to engage in community revitalization?

Conclusion

Bruce returned to help his friends find a better way of life. He developed friendships, and then, from those friendships, he was able to provide advice and direction to each individual. Bruce was successful in his endeavors. Several of his friends are now off the street, in transitional housing, and holding down jobs. God used Bruce to help revitalize his friends' lives.

We believe that God can use churches to help revitalize the lives of people through revitalizing communities. Some have given up on church because they fail to see the relevance of the church to their everyday life. Our experience has revealed four effective tactics:

1. Working to establish mutually responsible relationships in the community
2. Being open to learning from community members how they can be best served
3. Adjusting our expectations of when someone should be ready to take the next step
4. Most important, being open to the Holy Spirit's guidance

Using these four tactics, we can reestablish the church as a relevant part of the community by bringing health and healing to all people.

David B. Franklin is the lead pastor of Miracle City Seventh-day Adventist Church in Baltimore, Maryland. His church guides a coalition of community organizations seeking to revitalize the Frederick Avenue Corridor. Franklin from holds a bachelor of arts in business administration with an emphasis in marketing from Oakwood University and a master of divinity from the Seventh-day Adventist Theological Seminary at Andrews University. He is currently pursuing a doctorate in organizational development.

Transformational Impact:
A Journey to Relationships
Video Presentation (RT 13:59)
David Franklin

Chapter 2

Show Radical Hospitality:
Welcome Muslims in God's Name

Joseph Khabbaz and Gabriela Phillips

*"I say to you that many will come from the east and the west
and will take their places at the feast with Abraham,
Isaac and Jacob in the kingdom of heaven."*
—Matthew 8:11, NIV

Peering into the future, Jesus saw the day when the sons of Ishmael coming from the east and the children of Isaac coming from the west would gather at the welcoming table in sort of a much-anticipated family reunion. If this is our appointed future," I said, "why not practice such radical hospitality right here in North America?" I paused, wondering what would happen next. I was teaching a class to a church group, and the topic was cross-cultural mission in Atlanta.

In the third row, I saw that John, a middle-aged man, was visibly irritated. I had touched a raw nerve somewhere, and soon he retorted, "I have been deployed to Iraq; I know those people. We cannot be safe as long as they are free on our streets; we don't want them here. And do you want me to invite them to my home?"

Without thinking, I said, "Yes, but it's not my idea. It's God's! He said to love the enemy, and there is no better place than the table." Then I read aloud Matthew 8:11.

Some found my response amusing; John did not. Then I remembered what Warith, a refugee from Iraq, had said a few weeks before, "We Arab Muslims are a sort of litmus test among Christians in the West. The way the church responds will tell us if fear or the love of Jesus prevails."

Three months later, John called. I had forgotten this whole conversation, but he had not. That night, John had gone home and wrestled with God. In the presence of God, he was able to admit that he had been angry about having Muslims "taking over," and that anger had created a wall. He asked God for forgiveness and the courage to offer radical hospitality. A few days later, around his table was a Pakistani family moved to tears because they had been years in the US, and nobody had ever reached out to them. John found a brother in what used to be "the other" and felt free to love in ways he did not know were possible.

I asked a group of eight Iraqi refugees, "If you had the opportunity to speak to the Christians, what would you like them to know?"

"That we are lonely," one said.

"That we would rather have people coming to see us than their sofas," added another.

"That we are humans; we lost our homes and want to make America our home, but we can't if we are not accepted. That when we can host someone, we feel alive, that we have roots again, so we want them to be our guests . . ."

Hospitality, as an act of embrace, creates spaces in which the good news of the kingdom flourishes. "The theme of banqueting, of food and drink, is central in the ministry of Jesus. Was he not accused of being a glutton and a drunkard and of eating with sinners (Matt. 11:19)? Jesus was celebrating the messianic banquet but with all the wrong people!"[1] Eating, drinking, laughing, and growing all become acts of worship when done in the name of God. Zacchaeus found the path to God around the table. Mary—who probably would not be welcome in the public space considered male—grew as a disciple in the safety of her home.

The Greek word for "hospitality" is *philoxenia* (*philos*, loving, and *xenia*, strangers), or "love to strangers." It is a form of reconciliation that surpasses entertainment. So how does it appear as love to the stranger? What changes could radical hospitality generate?

Hospitality as a model for interfaith engagement

Hospitality is a powerful means for transforming relationships because it reconfigures the accepted boundaries between who is us and who is them. It is also a powerful biblical metaphor for salvation (see the Matthew 25 story of the great banquet and Revelation 3:20) and has the potential to heal by affirming the dignity of the suffering, enlarging the heart of the host, and letting the love of God become the binding cord between them.

Until now, our primary approach to Muslims has been through interfaith dialogue, in which each party seeks to affirm its propositional truths (the Trinity, Christ's divinity, the Incarnation, and the Cross). However, what if "presence" and solidarity in the midst of suffering, divine love as modeled in the triune relational mode of God's way of existing, what if the incarnation of "God with us" in the midst of chaos and the Cross as a place of self-sacrifice would proclaim our particular theology to a world in pain? What if divine hospitality were a window into God's biblical revelation? How differently would a refugee understand the Cross across the table of fellowship? What would such an experience bring into the life of the church?

Would a Muslim see the Trinity by the love it creates better than by the use of convoluted philosophical explanations of *ousia* and *hypostases*? Growth in our multifaith and multilayered communities means invested lives that lead to understanding, not the other way around. The outcome is no less truthful but situated in the context of life—holistic—and driven by the desire to love and receive truth, which is far superior to defending our belief system.

Because we are all guests of God's hospitality, we mirror His image when we extend hospitality to the stranger and turn the family table into a place for reconciliation. The Old Testament emphasis on eating and drinking in the presence of God speaks of feasting in ways that the fast pace of our societies has erased from our spiritual experience. It is important to make God central to this whole process. Speaking about the weather or the news may waste a precious opportunity to learn the story of the refugee before you. A useful question is, "When all this was happening to you, did you see the hand of God somewhere? Do you sense that perhaps God had a purpose beneath all your pain?"

When Muslims visit you, do not hesitate to pray before your meals. Address your prayers to God, not Jesus, and finish by saying, "In Your Name, we pray, amen." It is also good to raise your hand since this communicates to your neighbor that you are reaching out to God.

Jesus paid a high price for His "table manners." Christ's example creates tension at the center of His community. Are we, too, to follow the exclusionary logic of this world? Or should we adopt the embracing posture demonstrated at the cross even though it may result in being misunderstood by other Christians?

The rest of this chapter will seek an answer by portraying what it looks like to move in the direction of divine hospitality and exploring how you can make it possible in the life of your church. We will present a church-based model and a personal story to spark your imagination and to help you see yourself and your church writing the next stories.

Islam 101, hospitality, and lessons of a sojourner

In September 2019, I (Gaby) went to court with Samira. Many times, I had prayed with her for a favorable outcome on this very day and felt good about sharing comforting stories from Jesus. But this day, I did not expect to be confronted by God at the court. Because of an episode of domestic violence, she had ended up in a shelter and lost contact with her two children for more than a year. Now, here she was in court with basic English skills, sweating under an oversized headscarf, and struggling to navigate the complex legal system of the US. As the proceedings went on, I suddenly understood the gravity of the moment. She was about to lose custody of her children to foster care unless something radical happened in the next few minutes.

Discerning that God was knocking at my door, I texted my husband, and we agreed to have her and her kids move immediately into our home. On the way out of the courtroom, I wondered how we could financially afford three more people. God gave me a clear sign. Leaving the court, the parking clerk told me that I could go and did not have to pay the twelve-dollar parking fee. I asked God right there to teach my selfish heart the meaning of "it is more blessed to give than to receive" (Acts 20:35).

As a devout Muslim, Samira was grateful to live in a home where we prayed, abstained from pork and alcohol, and read the Bible. Her foundational beliefs are in God, angels, a long chain of prophets from Adam to Mohammad, and belief in the Bible, Qur'an, and the day of judgment. Unlike most Muslims, Samira thinks that the Bible is still valid and uncorrupted and that God dictated the Gospels to Jesus, the Torah to Moses, and the Psalms to David. She wakes up at five o'clock in the morning to pray and ritually wash. Samira loves repeating the name of God, for it brings her solace. She gets emotional when she hears about Jesus' mercy toward the stranger, especially the way He treated women. Often she says, "Now that we have broken the bread together, we are salt sisters." Food is her way to show love, and often, Samira wants to praise our kindness, so we redirect every praise to God and receive Samira's food as an expression of gratitude. She tells me that her food is clean, meaning that before she cooks, she invokes the name of God.

Speaking about God with Muslims is easy. We share common religious vocabulary: God, Allah, the Lord, the Almighty, the Most Merciful, and prayer (*du'a*) is core to both of us. The Qur'an, with its rich and diverse testimony about Jesus, creates a bridge to speak about His purity, mercy, power, and mission to cleanse us from sin. Jesus, for Muslims, is a powerful prophet. Sinless, He came miraculously from a virgin and will return one day. Samira's eschatology is messy, and so is her belief about what happens at the grave, so the best way to address these matters is by allowing the Bible to speak for itself.

Seeing God's offer of redemption through the lenses of the powerless and excluded has awakened in our family a renewed love and gratitude for God. Jesus is not an abstract philosophical construct but a male Protector whose wisdom and power could heal women who have experienced abuse and rejection. Jesus models forgiveness that is humanly impossible. Asking Samira to extend this forgiveness against those who have hurt her has challenged me to reconsider my standing with some people whom I have written off.

Because of her Islamic background, Samira sees Jesus as a powerful broker before God. Time will heal that understanding so that she can see that both are on the same side. Recently she has joined our study group on the Bible, and her hunger for God keeps challenging my apathy. I thought I was helping Samira. God knew that she was helping me. We are sojourning daily closer to Him, one meal at a time, one story at a time.

How to start a refugee support ministry at your church:
A pastor's perspective

Since 2017, the Sligo Seventh-day Adventist Church has been helping refugee families from Syria, Iraq, Afghanistan, Yemen, Sudan, and Ethiopia by furnishing apartments, and providing needed groceries, home goods, and school supplies for children. During that time, we have had the privilege of meeting more than 50 refugee families and over 250 individuals who were once strangers but whom we now call friends. By God's grace, the Sligo Refugee Support Ministry has been able to distribute well over a thousand items to refugee families in need. Before you start a refugee support ministry in your church, assess the situation and learn about the people.

Assess the assets of both your church and refugee families. When it comes to supporting refugees in our communities, we need to ensure that we start with accurate assumptions. If your church begins with the position that resettled refugees are a problem that needs fixing, they can inadvertently assign labels that are not helpful—terms such as *illegal immigrants* or *extremists*. These sensationalized labels create a disconnect between the church community and refugee families.

ADRA International highlights the fact that "seeking asylum in other countries is a human right recognized by Article 14 of the Universal Declaration of Human Rights. Countries that have ratified the 1951 Refugee Convention are obligated to protect refugees in their territory."[2]

Furthermore, the 1951 UN Refugee Convention (and its 1967 Protocol) asserts, "A refugee should not be returned to a country where they face serious threats to their life or freedom. This is now considered a rule of customary international law."[3]

As proposed by Asset Based Community Development advocates,[4] the best way to transform a community is to ask the question, "What can this community do itself to achieve its own goals and dreams?" Many refugee families that we have met through Sligo's Refugee Support Ministry are highly skilled and motivated, and they desire to use their life experiences to create a better future for themselves here in the United States. We have visited with electrical engineers, veterinarians, business owners, chefs, and scientists who have a tremendous degree of skill and intellectual capital. Through our ministry, we have met numerous families and individuals, and in each case, without exception, the refugees share how grateful they are to the United States for granting them refuge.

As a result, the Sligo's Refugee Support Ministry seeks to use the gifts and talents that God has already given refugee families and connect them with the gifts and talents of our church members. Such an approach focuses on meeting the needs of refugee families while not forgetting the gifts that those refugees have to offer. In all our outreach projects, the refugee families themselves help create networks, provide translation, assist with distribution, and give care to families who need support.

Here are some questions you can ask when assessing the assets of your church and the refugee families you feel called to support.[5]

- Have we completed an asset map in our community to see what organizations our church can join or partner with to access resources?
- How can we create a space to listen to refugee families and find out what they want to change?
- How can we use the gifts and talents of refugee families through participation in the church's outreach program?
- Have we created a plan with church volunteers for enlisting their gifts and talents to energize and mobilize the congregation?

Know your state. Before starting a refugee support ministry in your church, you will need to evaluate the refugee landscape of your state and get a better understanding of refugee trends in your ministry context.

A great source of information is The Refugee Processing Center (RPC).

RPC is operated by the US Department of State (DOS) Bureau of Population, Refugees, and Migration (PRM) in the Rosslyn section of Arlington, Virginia, USA. Using the free interactive reporting tool on the RPC website, your church can identify how many refugees have been admitted into your state.[6]

Following is a report that was generated on the RPC website. It presents the number of refugee arrivals by each state.

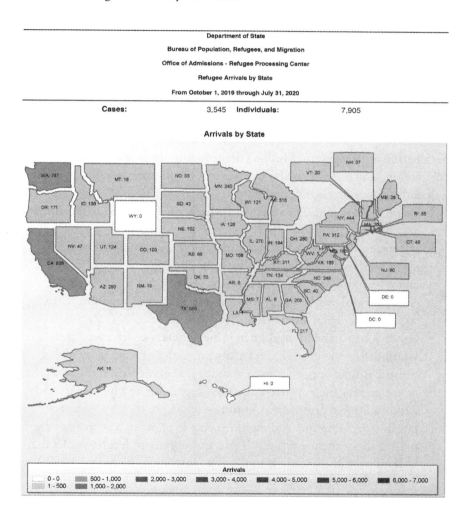

Hospitality and hummus. Those who volunteered in the Sligo Refugee Support Ministry found that friendships with refugee families began and grew very quickly. We also discovered that as we served them, they considered us their friends instantly, as generosity is an important value in their culture.

As a result, when our volunteers dropped off a welcome bag, home goods, or school supplies, the refugee families would often seek to reciprocate. They would often invite the volunteers for dinner or encourage them to return for a meal at a more convenient time. We noticed that refugee families felt indebted to return the "favor" because of the generosity they experienced through our Sligo Refugee Support Ministry.

As we extended hospitality to our guests, these refugee families were able to express their appreciation, which is an essential virtue for anyone with a good reputation in the Middle East. Our volunteers found having a meal with a refugee family fun, yet they felt apprehensive because many of them had never been personally invited to a Muslim's home for dinner. Stories of their visits are enlightening and noteworthy for any Adventist volunteer wanting to neighbor well with refugees in their community.[7]

Here are some practical tips based on what we have learned at the dinners:

- Beverages: We never stayed long in a home without being offered something to drink. Our hosts gave the choice of coffee or tea, and it was expected that guests would accept what was offered. As Adventists might not drink coffee or tea, it is considered proper to request water as an alternative.
- Food: When arriving for dinner, it is customary to have a conversation before the meal. Expect a large quantity of food to be served because it is an opportunity to demonstrate generosity and respect to the guests. The appetizers are often vegetarian and include a salad with traditional dips such as hummus (chickpea dip) or baba ghanoush (eggplant dip.) You should expect the host to have prepared a meat dish for the main meal. If you are vegetarian, feel free to let the host know at the time of accepting the invitation. Note that Muslims are forbidden to eat pork or drink alcohol.
- Etiquette: It is important to sit correctly and not slouch. When saying hello or goodbye to someone, it is essential to shake hands. When a man is introduced to a Muslim woman, the choice should be left to the women whether to shake hands or not. It is also customary to take off your shoes before entering the house as prayer

(*salaat*) often takes place on the living room floor. Encourage your church volunteers to dress modestly when visiting a Muslim's home. Out of respect, volunteers should cover their shoulders and knees. Also, do not be surprised if Muslim women do not want you to take a photo. It is considered impolite to take a picture of a woman without first asking.

Conversation starters. When spending time with a refugee family, what can you talk about with the hosts? Here are some ideas:

- Ask them about their family both in the United States and abroad.
- Talk about their lifestyle, including their favorite foods and how they are prepared.
- Prayer is essential to a Muslim's faith. Ask them what prayer means to them and about its significance in their lives.
- Ask about their journey as refugees and how God watched over them as they resettled in a new land.
- Ask them how their children are doing in school and how they are settling in to the new academic institution.
- Many refugee families use the smart application Google Translate to communicate. Feel free to practice English with the family, as many refugee families would like to enhance their English skills.

Build a team.[8] As a pastor, you understand the need for sustainable ministry in your local church. We have all been there when the initial excitement and enthusiasm of a new ministry energizes the congregation, but after a few months, you feel like you are the only one with the hand to the plow, pleading for people to help. Building a team is essential for your church to impact the lives of refugees positively over a sustained period.

Here are some steps to build a refugee support ministry in your church:

1. Choose your team. Find people in your church who have a passion for serving refugees and have the best intentions. Young adults in your church are a great source of drive and skill when it comes to getting behind a worthy cause in the community. Connect with your church outreach coordinator, Adventist Community Service representative, and other local nongovernmental organizations who may already be supporting refugees in your area. Ask local pastors in the area if their

church would like to collaborate with you.

2. Get it on your calendar. Put team meeting dates on a calendar straight away. Schedule them every month, and set aside one to two hours.

3. Make a task list. Assign a team member the responsibility of creating a task list at the end of each meeting. The task list should include a description of the task to complete by the next meeting and the name of the person responsible for the task.

4. Set accountability. Choose some team members to follow up with the others to ensure the tasks are completed by the next meeting.

Useful Resources

Books and Journal Articles

Annan, Kent. *You Welcomed Me: Loving Refugees and Immigrants*. Downers Grove, IL: IVP Books, 2018.

George, Sam, and Miriam Adeney. *Refugee Diaspora: Missions Amid the Greatest Humanitarian Crisis of the World*. Littleton, CO: William Carey Publishing, 2018.

Nydell, Margaret K. *Understanding Arabs: A Guide for Westerners*. Yarmouth, ME: Intercultural Press, 2005.

Pohl, Christine D. *Making Room: Recovering Hospitality as a Christian Tradition*. Grand Rapids, MI: W. B. Eerdmans, 1999.

Roennfeldt, Peter, and Nathan Brown. *If You Can Eat . . . You Can Make Disciples: Sharing Faith in a Multi-Faith World*. Warburton, Victoria, Australia: Signs Publishing, 2018.

Ross, Cathy. "Creating Space: Hospitality as a Metaphor for Mission." *Anvil* 25, no. 3, 2008. https://biblicalstudies.org.uk/pdf/anvil/25-3_167.pdf.

Samaan, Philip G. *Abraham's Other Son: Islam Among Judaism & Christianity*. Collegedale, TN: College Press, 2012.

Smucker, Shawn. *Once We Were Strangers: What Friendship With a Syrian Refugee Taught Me About Loving My Neighbor.* Grand Rapids, MI: Revell, 2018.

Adventist Institutions

- ADRA. https://adra.org.
  - World Refugee Sabbath resources, including sermon notes and social media posts
  - A documentary created by ADRA.EU
- Adventist Community Services. http://www.communityservices.org/refugees.
  - Refugee Awareness Sabbath program ideas and activities
  - Ideas for starting a refugee ministry in your church
  - Practical ways to reach out to refugees
- NAD Ministerial Compassion Movement. http://compassionmovement.org.
- Adventist Refugee and Immigrant Ministries. https://www.refugeeministries.com.
- World Relief Site. https://worldreliefdupageaurora.org/stories-news/6-ways-welcome-refugees-immigrants.
- Adventist Muslim Friendly Association (AMFA). https://www.amfa4refugees.com/.

Media resources

- Evangelical Immigration Table, a website that explains the root cause of the current crisis in the US and what Christians can do. http://evangelicalimmigrationtable.com/.

Sligo Adventist Church Refugee Support Ministry bulletin inserts:

On April 6th, the Sligo Refugee Support Ministry will be providing Care Boxes with much needed supplies. We need your help filling these boxes with the following items in order to assist 25 families.

- Toothpaste & brushes
- Large cans of powdered milk
- Garbanzo beans (chick peas)
- Lentils
- Salt
- Tahini

Where: You can drop these items off at the Sligo Office during the week between the hours of 9 am and 5 pm from Monday to Thursday, or 9 am and 12 pm on Fridays. Otherwise you can bring your items to the Memorial Chapel.

Where: Volunteers will meet at Sligo Church to distribute the items on April 6th for departure at 3:00 pm.

PLEASE RSVP IF YOU PLAN TO ATTEND

NAME:

PHONE:

EMAIL:

REFUGEE SUPPORT MINISTRY

The Sligo Church Refugee Support Ministry is kicking off an initiative called the "Back2School Drive." You can take part in helping 150 refugee kids start the upcoming school year with their best foot forward. Read on to learn how!

How We Can Help: From now until August 8th you can help by donating a backpack with school supplies and dropping them off at the Sligo Church office from Monday to Thursday, 9 AM to 5 PM. Friday 9 AM to 12PM.

- Backpack – Boy
- Backpack – Girl
- Water Bottle
- Colored pencils
- Markers
- Pencils #2 Lead
- Eraser
- Ruler
- Glue Stick
- Scissors
- Notebook

When: Volunteers will meet at Sligo Church to distribute the items on August 10th for departure at 3:00pm.

If you would also like to participate in the presentation of the backpacks to the refugee families, feel free to complete the form below and place in the offering plate at the end of the service today!

PLEASE RSVP IF YOU PLAN TO ATTEND

NAME:

PHONE:

EMAIL:

Sligo Adventist Church Refugee Support Ministry Welcome Bag given with supplies to refugee families.

But the command, "Go ye into all the world," is not to be lost sight of. We are called upon to lift our eyes to the "regions beyond." Christ tears away the wall of partition, the dividing prejudice of nationality, and teaches a love for all the human family. He lifts men from the narrow circle which their selfishness prescribes; He abolishes all territorial lines and artificial distinctions of society. He makes no difference between neighbors and strangers, friends and enemies. He teaches us to look upon every needy soul as our brother, and the world as our field.

—Ellen G. White, *The Desire of Ages*, 823

Compassion card design: This gives the volunteers who put together the welcome kit an opportunity to write a message.

Welcome to the United States!

We pray that the God of all mercy and love will be with you and your family!

Welcome to the United States!

My name is _____ and I had the pleasure of putting your Welcome Kit together. I hope that each of the items provided will be a blessing to you and your family.

My prayers are with you and know that our loving God will be your source of strength and provision to you as your make your home here.

God bless you!

1. Cathy Ross, "Creating Space: Hospitality as a Metaphor for Mission," *Anvil* 25, no. 3 (2008): 168, https://biblicalstudies.org.uk/pdf/anvil/25-3_167.pdf.

2. "Get the Facts: Refugees and IDPs," ADRA, May 2, 2016, https://adra.org/beyond-the-crisis-global-refugee-facts/.

3. "The 1951 Refugee Convention," UNHCR, accessed July 7, 2020, https://www.unhcr.org/pages/49da0e466.html.

4. Jay Van Gronigen, CRWRC, and Communities First, "An Introduction to Asset Based Community Development for Church Leaders," Christian Reformed World Relief Committee, accessed July 7, 2020, https://peoplevine.blob.core.windows.net/media/451/introtoabcd forchurchleaders1.pdf.

5. Gronigen, CRWRC, and Communities First, [9].

6. You can find the reporting tool on the Refugee Processing Center website at https://ireports.wrapsnet.org/Interactive-Reporting/EnumType/Report?ItemPath=/rpt_WebArrivals Reports/Map%20-%20Arrivals%20by%20State%20and%20Nationality.

7. See Margaret K. Nydell, *Understanding Arabs: a Guide for Westerners* (Boston, MA: Intercultural Press, 2000).

8. See Kara Eckmann Powell and Brad M. Griffin, *Sticky Faith Launch Kit: Your Next 180 Days Toward Sticky Faith* (Fuller Youth Institute, 2013).

Joseph Khabbaz, MDiv, is the vice-president for spiritual life and chaplain at Southern Adventist University. Previously, he served as the pastor for youth and young adults at Sligo Seventh-day Adventist Church in Takoma Park, Maryland. Sligo Church's refugee support ministry has helped sustain more than forty families and 250 people in the state of Maryland for the past three years.

Gabriela Phillips serves as Adventist Muslim Relations coordinator for the North American Division. For the past twenty years, she and her husband, Marty, have dedicated their lives to building bridges between Adventist and Muslims for the purpose of growing in saving faith. She is currently pursuing a doctorate in intercultural studies focusing on faith development in context.

Refugees in the Room
Video Presentation (RT: 21:25)
Gabriela Phillips

Chapter 3

Make the Church Accessible and Safe for Children and Their Families

Daron Pratt

Our children are in crisis. They are constantly bombarded by a wide range of technology and impacted by cultural change, much of it negative. Modern affluent societies overflow with a range of goods produced for the entertainment, pleasure, convenience, and education of our children. Children are firmly in the sights of corporations with a barrage of marketing and advertising designed to capture this multibillion-dollar market, yet something is wrong. The current generation of children is more stressed; less content; and less healthy physically, socially, and mentally than any other generation. Sharon Beder writes that "the consequence of this corporate capture of childhood has been a generation of children who have been manipulated, shaped, and exploited as never before in history. Not only have they lost the opportunity to play and develop at their own pace, their psyches have been damaged and their view of the world distorted. . . . Children have never been under such pressure to 'succeed, conform and look good.' "[1] The stresses that children and families are under today interfere with their discipleship journey, and the church needs to respond in creative and relevant ways to reach this generation.

Our churches are in crisis. Researchers suggest that between 60 percent and, in some cases, 90 percent of the children who currently attend your church will leave it. Many will decide to do this before they reach their teenage years.[2]

These statistics are juxtaposed against the words of Jesus, who instructs us to let the children come to Him and do not hinder them. The task for churches, schools, and families to disciple and retain our children is huge. When are we going to wake up and take the words of Jesus seriously? We need to aim lower, much lower than we previously have, if we are going to reach children and their families.

Children and their families must be prioritized everywhere—in our programs, our budgets, our service activities, our mentoring, and our mission! Loving the children in the 4–14 window is the key. Do we know them by name, both in and outside the church? Do we affirm them? Do we include them in our worship services? Do they feel like they belong? Are our programs and initiatives truly intergenerational? Dead men's tales just do not cut it when it comes to our children.

Equipping parents is also essential. Children are likely to be as faithful as their parents are. This means that we need to equip our parents to be the best spiritual "disciplers" they can be. How are we, as a church, prioritizing parents in our discipleship ministries? Are children and families our great commission or great omission?

We must also learn to make every effort to welcome, tolerate, and include children in our corporate worship. If I do not hear a baby crying in a church service, then I know that church is dying. Children are a sign—when we welcome children into worship, we welcome the very presence of Jesus. What would happen if we dared to assume that children have the same rights to the sights, sounds, touches, tastes, and smells of worship as adults? What would happen if we intentionally welcomed children into worship? As we begin to think about what it means to welcome children to worship, here are some important aspects to consider.

Excellence in ministry to the 4–14 window

We know that children are more likely to make a lifelong decision to follow Jesus sometime during what is known as the 4–14 window. This window is an age bracket, and it is indeed one of the largest unreached people groups on the planet.

It is interesting to note that most church congregations devote 80 percent of their budget dollars to adult ministries, while only 10–20 percent goes to children and family ministries.[3] More dedicated and consistent investment in children and families could well be the first step to reversing the alarming statistics of loss found in almost all our churches.

Eighty percent of all who find Christ do so by the age of fourteen; 90 percent by age twenty-five. This has been labeled the 4–14 window of opportunity.[4] Children are also more likely than adults to evangelize their friends. The church has often targeted adults with evangelistic outreach. However, research indicates that reversing the current funding is likely to result not only in our children making lifelong decisions for Christ but also in evangelistic kingdom growth.

It thus makes sense that if children are more likely to respond to the gospel than adults, children's facilities should be the best that we can offer. Rather than being a gloomy, run-down room or building at the back of the church, our children's facilities should be large and well lit, have appropriate amenities, and be creatively decorated. These types of facilities are more likely to be full of children, along with their families. In my ministry, I have found from trial and error that the larger the room and the more cared for and equipped that room is, the higher the number of children and their parents who attend will be. I have seen churches revolutionized and revitalized just because they chose to prioritize children and families. On the other hand, among the biggest factors inhibiting church growth are poorly maintained children's facilities and inadequate parking.

Children's Ministries research revealed that families place a premium on the children's ministry experience of their kids. The majority (66 percent) said the children's ministry program was "very important" in their overall consideration when they chose their current church. Parents ranked "the Children's Ministry" as the third most important reason they joined their current church—only marginally behind "the church's emphasis" and "preaching." "Your children's ministry is a growth engine for church growth."[5]

Excellence in children's programming is also important. We can run all the "cute" programs we like and entertain to our heart's content. We can use all of the latest technology and gadgets. However, we must remember that the aim of all programs and ministries is to change lives and help our children along the discipleship journey. Children need adult mentors in their lives who are committed to the long haul with these children rather than just a passing phase. Churches need to staff their children's ministries first, and with their most talented members, rather than just plugging holes. Our children need staff who have a big heart for God and a big heart for children. Children identify with the significant mentors in their lives and hang on their every word. If we want eternal values to be in our children's hearts, then they have to be in ours first. Staff mentors must be authentic and committed. Children can spot hypocrisy a mile off, and it is one of the biggest disrupters to their discipleship journey.

These are key performance indicators of 4–14 window churches:

- Invest significantly in the 4–14 window
- Prioritize children and families everywhere
- Renovate and refurbish their children and family spaces

Activate the church

In our modern culture, children frequently find themselves disconnected from the community around them for various reasons. Family breakups and/or busy parents often mean our children find themselves home alone for extended periods. The myriad of modern technologies, including social media, the internet, gaming, iPods, and laptops, means that children can now access most things from their bedrooms at home with little need to venture to a library, shopping center, or other public space. The resulting individuation and loss of connection and mentors mean that now, more than ever, the church needs to see itself as an interactive community that connects the people in its congregation in intergenerational activities and programs. Adventurer and Pathfinder clubs are two of the best mentoring, intergenerational, and evangelistic programs that the church offers, and we would do well to connect every family to these groups intentionally.

We also must make sure that every church program is intergenerational because this is where the faith of our children develops best. Reggie Joiner, author of *Think Orange*, says, "The Church has a unique opportunity to connect kids with Christian adults who will value them enough to help them interpret life, support them in times of tragedy, and carry them through life transitions."[6] Benjamin Lundquist believes that "withing" is key to faith transmission. "Mentoring is deeper 'withing.' " "We don't need to teach them, just hang out together on the curb, give them authority to make decisions, give them clarity of purpose, and give them intergenerational consistency."[7]

Jerome Berryman says that what children experience in church is what they associate with Christianity.[8] This means that what we expose our children to in church is crucial to faith transmission and long-term commitment to the church, its ministry, and mission.

This is why it is important that we intentionally make our worship services intergenerational, welcoming, and accessible for children and families. I believe that something is seriously wrong when a family that has been separated and busy during the week arrives in church only to separate for their age-related activity, then meet up again after church for the trip home. While age-targeted activities are beneficial and necessary, corporate intergenerational worship on a regular basis is a must. Intergenerational worship is a strong formative agent for everyone, so we need to ensure that what we do in worship is relevant and nurtures the kind of people we want our children and ourselves to be.

John Westerhoff writes, "If our children are to have faith, they must have opportunities to worship with the adults of the church. Worship is not only a time when the content of faith is delivered, but also a time when our churches communicate the feelings, subtle nuances, and transcendent meanings of faith."[9]

When families attend worship services together, children see their parents identifying with the church family and prioritizing their faith. Children watch their parents and others sing, pray, and give of their resources. Observing these rituals has a positive effect on the long-term discipleship of children.

Kara Powell and Chap Clark found in their *Sticky Faith* research that our children and teens flourish when we surround them with a minimum of five significant adults who can speak into their lives. These are adults whom we trust, who know them by name and stand for the same ideals and values that we as parents stand for. Further, Powell and Clark discovered that there is a strong correlation between children attending all-age intergenerational worship and sticky faith. This finding is as close as their research came to finding the "silver bullet" in developing a faith that sticks for our children and teens.[10]

A church that welcomes children will make an effort to structure its worship space and liturgy to include children in the worship event as a matter of routine, not as an occasional, special-event, cute factor. It is not easy to create these sorts of worship services, but when we are creative and considerate, we can create worship services that nurture the faith of every church member.

David Csinos and Ivy Beckwith say that discipleship is about "walking alongside children on the path of discipleship, apprenticing them into the way that Jesus laid out for all of us. We who work with children are disciples, just like those young people in our midst. We are formed as disciples even as we form others. Children and adults walk the path together as equals on a common journey of discipleship."[11]

Intentional intergenerational churches will also create intergenerational play-and-pray areas in their worship spaces where children can quietly do activities as they listen and interact with what is happening in worship. Often these activities are based on the themes for the day, and this allows the children to create, reflect on, and internalize the themes.

Ed Stetzer, director of LifeWay Research, said, "Teens are looking for more from a youth ministry than a holding tank with pizza. . . . They look for a church that teaches them how to live life. As they enter young adulthood, church involvement that has made a difference in their lives gives them a powerful reason to keep attending."[12] We, the church, need to make sure that we give our children and families a myriad of reasons to keep attending church. This means being friendly, relevant, welcoming, and inclusive of children and families everywhere.

Another significant welcoming opportunity that the whole church body is ideally placed to provide is that of mentoring and influencing our children. We need to remember that Deuteronomy was written to the whole Israelite community and not just to parents. It does take a village to raise a child, and the church is in the unique position to be the "village" that provides positive role models who take an interest in the children of the church and promote the same values that the parents are promoting. Lifeway Research, again, says, "Teens who had at least one adult from church make a significant time investment in their lives also were more likely to keep attending church. More of those who stayed in the church—by a margin of 46 percent to 28 percent—said five or more adults at church had invested time with them personally and spiritually."[13]

These are key performance indicators of 4–14 window churches:

- Get the whole church together for at least 50–80 percent of their church activities
- Make sure that they know every child by name and make sure that every child has at least one extra safe mentor besides their parents
- Provide multisensory, intergenerational, welcoming worship spaces for everyone to worship together

Sending it home: Take-home packs

If the church is truly going to impact those in the 4–14 window, then both what happens at church and what happens at home need to be consistent and synergized. To achieve this, parents need to be informed and equipped to teach and reinforce what their children are being taught at church. Our job as a church is to make the job of spiritual parenting as easy as possible.

One strategy is a "take-home pack" for parents from either the main worship service or the child's Sabbath School. These packs can consist of questions, discussion points, or activities based on the week's curriculum or the topic of the main church service. Parents can choose some or all of the activities to do with their children during the week. This strategy will help families to form habits centered on regular spiritual time together and will support the parents' role as the primary spiritual mentors of their child. The take-home packs also provide parents with the confidence they need to start spiritual conversations and identify teachable moments with their child. These activities do not need to be long or detailed. Anything the parent does of a spiritual nature with their child is, in fact, more important than anything done at church.

When we prioritize our families and give them practical ideas to build and nurture spirituality in the home, we help them grow and help them see that being a Christian means living it 24-7 in all aspects of their lives.

These are key performance indicators of 4–14 window churches:

- Support and equip parents as the primary faith transmitters
- Create take-home resources to reinforce faith
- Create partnerships between church, home, and mentors

The power of memory events

The church can welcome and include children by providing special memory events that include the whole family. What children want most is time with their parents. Memory events provide a supportive atmosphere where this can occur. Very few families have time to play together, yet play is part of the process that holds families together and strengthens them. Church-organized family memory events encourage bonding within families and provide a model for families to follow at home. When a church organizes regular family memory events, families sense that the church values them and, consequently, their commitment to God, the church, and one another grows.

Some ideas for special family memory events include family breakfasts; barbecues; movie nights; sports events; father-son events; mother-daughter events; family camps; beach days; visits to a zoo, national park, or farm; pool days; craft nights; or a men's shed. The ideas are endless, but the rewards are of eternal significance. Family memory events also help newer members and interests because they encourage members to get to know each other on an informal basis and help families to feel more at ease with other church members.

When young people are asked to recall their spiritual journey and the high points, often the church family memory events are listed as some of the most significant spiritual moments. Family play and memory events provide anchor points on the discipleship journey upon which our children can hang their faith. Family play and memory events open the door to the sacred and, indeed, to what the Sabbath is meant to be. It is vital that all families find time to "Sabbath" together, and if a church can facilitate this, then families will thank you for it. Marva Dawn writes about the value of "one day of the week in which we cease working and focus on resting, embracing the values of God's kingdom, and feasting. . . . I cannot emphasize enough the positive changes it brings to our hectic lives when we faithfully reserve an entire Sabbath day set apart to deepen our relationships with God and family."[14]

These are key performance indicators for 4–14 window churches:

- Create significant memory events for their families
- Program less so that families can "Sabbath" more
- Intentionally welcome and include families

Service with compassion

Research by the Search Institute has found that family service activities have a significant impact on the spiritual life of our children.[15] Tim and Alison Simpson write, "When children see their parents selflessly giving of their money, time and resources, they learn to orient their own lives the same way. . . . When a family learns to put others first and to give, it beautifully transforms the culture of the household."[16] Churches can organize service projects in which families can safely participate. Meaningful service projects are designed so that each member of the family feels that he or she is contributing. These kinds of activities not only help the community in need but also grow the faith of children exponentially. Service activities could involve yard cleanup for the elderly and sick, visits to nursing homes, food drives, soup kitchens, community feeding programs, mission trips either domestically or overseas, or collecting for charities.

Another advantage of families serving others is that it breaks down the barriers between the church and the community. Many churches shut their children into their church programs and church schools, creating a fortress mentality to protect their children from the evil world. The gospel commission requires us to be salt and light, and to go out into the world, understand the culture, evaluate the needs, and minister to those needs. We do a disservice to our children when we cloister them in a fortress. The church needs to model loving care and concern for the world in which it lives and involve our families in that care and concern. The benefits for all are of eternal significance.

This is a key performance indicator for 4–14 window churches:

- Create service activities that involve everyone.

Take every decision seriously

Too many times, I hear the cry of "they are too young," or "they are not ready," or even that children are incapable of making a decision for Jesus. I hear too many stories of children being ignored, overlooked, or turned away, and this is tragic! The 4–14 window is open for only a short time. Unless we are strategic and active during this time frame, we are likely to lose them! The kingdom of heaven belongs to children, and it is high time that we, as a church and as individuals, begin to take this mandate of Jesus seriously!

You are in a dangerous place if you get between a child and Jesus. We need to lead them, mentor them, champion them, and learn from them. Discipleship is a two-way street. It is time to move beyond the statistics and think about where we spend our budget dollars and resources. Children aged four to fourteen are where we need to do better as a church, especially when it comes to evangelism and discipleship.

Do children in your church have a place at the table? Do our children get a place at the mission, evangelism, or discipleship table? Do they get their fair share of the budget pie? Do we take their decisions and discipleship seriously?

Researcher George Barna, the author of *Transforming Children Into Spiritual Champions*, stresses the importance of children's ministry, contending that lifelong moral views are largely in place by adolescence. The concrete is setting by the age of nine. "What you believe at age 13 is pretty much what you're going to die believing," Barna said. Research compiled by the Barna Group shows that children between the ages of five and thirteen have a 32 percent probability of accepting Jesus Christ as their Savior. That likelihood drops to 4 percent for teenagers between the ages of fourteen and eighteen and ticks back up to 6 percent for adults older than eighteen.[17]

It is a discipleship window too!

Children's ministry is an optimal way to shape the church's rising leadership. In a 2003 Barna Group nationwide survey of pastors, church staff, and lay leaders, four of five leaders said they participated in church children's programs for several years before they turned thirteen. It is also interesting that most of those who are involved in leadership—pastoral and other leadership roles in the church—served and observed alongside their parents, participated, and were discipled along the way.

Finally, when a child does decide for Christ, please, please, please take it seriously. The 4–14 window is open for only a brief time. If we do not take this opportunity seriously, ignore, or even worse, do not accept a child's decision, then we are poor stewards of the gospel commission.

These are key performance indicators of 4–14 window churches:

- Take every decision for Jesus seriously, especially when a child makes a decision
- Ask for decisions regularly
- Baptize children generally before they leave the 4–14 window

Useful Resources

Books

Barna, George. *Transforming Children Into Spiritual Champions.* Ventura, CA: Regal Books, 2003.

Beder, Sharon. *This Little Kiddy Went to Market: The Corporate Capture of Childhood.* N.p.: UNSW Press, 2009.

Bengston, Vern L., Norella M. Putney, and Susan C. Harris. *Families and Faith: How Religion Is Passed Down Across Generations.* New York: Oxford University Press, 2013.

Csinos, David, and Ivy Beckwith. *Children's Ministries in the Way of Jesus.* Downer's Grove, IL: InterVarsity, 2013.

Dawn, Marva J. *Is It a Lost Cause? Having the Heart of God for the Church's Children.* Grand Rapids, MI: Eerdmans, 1997.

Joiner, Reggie. *Think Orange: Imagine the Impact When Church and Family Collide.* Colorado Springs, CO: David Cook Publications, 2009.

Kinnaman, David. *Unchristian: What a New Generation Really Thinks About Christianity . . . And Why It Matters.* Grand Rapids, MI: Baker Books, 2007.

Powell, Kara, and Chap Clark. *Sticky Faith: Everyday Ideas to Build Lasting Faith in Your Kids.* Grand Rapids, MI: Zondervan, 2011.

Powell, Kara, Jake Mulder, and Brad Griffin. *Growing Young: 6 Essential Strategies to Help Young People Discover and Love Your Church.* Grand Rapids, MI: Baker Books, 2016.

Simpson, Tim, and Alison Simpson. *Amazing Adventures, Creative Connections, and Daring Deeds: 40 Ideas That Put Feet to Your Family's Faith.* Colorado Springs, CO: Navpress, 2010.

Westerhoff, John M. *Will Our Children Have Faith?* San Francisco: Harper and Row, 1976.

1. Sharon Beder, *This Little Kiddy Went to Market: The Corporate Capture of Childhood* (n.p.: UNSW Press, 2009), 9.

2. See George Barna, *Transforming Children Into Spiritual Champions: Why Children Should Be Your Church's #1 Priority* (Ventura, CA: Regal Books, 2003).

3. See Barna Group, Inc. https://www.barna.com.

4. See the 4/14 Movement website at https://414movement.com/.

5. See Jennifer Hooks, "Children's Ministry's Impact on Your Church Growth," childrensministry.com, https://childrensministry.com/childrens-ministrys-impact-church-growth.

6. Reggie Joiner, *Think Orange: Imagine the Impact When Church and Family Collide* (Colorado Springs, CO: David Cook Publications, 2009), 73.

7. Benjamin Lundquist, AUC Ministries Meeting, 2018.

8. Jerome Berryman, "Godly Play and the Language of Christian Faith," *Christian Century*, March 27, 2019, https://www.christiancentury.org/article/features/godly-play-and-language -christian-faith.

9. John M. Westerhoff, *Will Our Children Have Faith?* (San Francisco: Harper and Row, 1976).

10. See Kara Powell and Chap Clark, *Sticky Faith: Everyday Ideas to Build Lasting Faith in Your Kids* (Grand Rapids, MI: Zondervan, 2011).

11. David Csinos and Ivy Beckwith, *Children's Ministry in the Way of Jesus* (Downers Grove, IL: InterVarsity, 2013), 61

12. "Parents and Churches Can Help Teens Stay in Church," LifeWay Research, August 7, 2007, https://lifewayresearch.com/2007/08/07/parents-churches-can-help-teens-stay-in-church/.

13. "Parents and Churches."

14. Marva J. Dawn, *Is It a Lost Cause? Having the Heart of God for the Church's Children* (Grand Rapids, MI: Eerdmans, 1997), 120, 121.

15. See the Search Institute website at https://www.search-institute.org/.

16. Tim Simpson and Alison Simpson, *Amazing Adventures, Creative Connections and Daring Deeds: 40 Ideas That Put Feet to Your Family's Faith* (Colorado Springs, CO: Navpress, 2010), 11.

17. See Barna Group, Inc., https://www.barna.com; John W. Kennedy, "The 4–14 Window," *Christianity Today*, July 1, 2004, https://www.christianitytoday.com/ct/2004/july/37.53.html.

Daron Pratt, BA, MA in theology, has been a children's pastor for the past twenty-six years and is currently the Family and Children's Ministries director for the North New South Wales Conference in Australia. Pratt's passion for children's ministry and evangelism is contagious, and he travels the world to gain resources in this area.

The Four to Fourteen Window
Video Presentation (RT: 19:51)
Daron Pratt

ACTION 2—SERVE

Multiply through engaging

all members in ministry

and mission.

I Want to Play!

Jose Cortes Jr.

God has given each of you a gift from his great variety of spiritual gifts.
Use them well to serve one another.
—1 Peter 4:10, NLT

The softball game between pastors and youth is a tradition at the Greater New York Conference Hispanic camp meeting. I was the new Youth Ministries director, and I love baseball, so I was ready to play! I remember I wore my jersey, the one my wife had given to me, with my last name, "Cortes," on the back and a big #1. (Remember, it was a gift from my wife. I am glad she thinks I am #1.) I had forgotten my glove and bat at home in Long Island, so the night before, after all the programming at the Youth and Young Adult tent was over, I had driven home to get my baseball equipment. I was ready to play.

As I got to the field, I made my way toward the youth team; after all, I was the Youth director. Soon I heard the voice of my conference president. "Jose, you are a pastor, you need to be on our team." When the conference president calls, you tend to pay attention, so I did and slowly walked to the other side of the field, where the pastors were gathering and strategically working on the lineup. It was almost like a science. They had to win this game!

As I got there, my conference president asked, "Jose, what position do you play?"

"Center field," I replied.

"That's taken. Pastor Mejia plays center field."

"Well, I can do third base."

"No, Angel Rodriguez has third."

"How about second base."

"Plinio Cruz plays second; it's taken."

"First?"

"No, Hernandez has got that."

"Shortstop?"

"No, I am the shortstop."

I backed away from that one quickly; you do not want to play the same position as your president.

After going through all the positions and seeing that every single one was taken, my conference president said to me, "Hey, do catcher."

That was the one position my dad had always told me—since I was a little kid—not ever to play. I hate catching!

As I headed back behind the plate, feeling kind of humiliated, to assume my position as catcher, he added, "Jose, we are missing a glove here in the infield. This is slow pitch softball; you are the catcher. You really don't need a glove; please give us your glove."

I gave up my glove and got behind home plate, really fearful of a foul tip to my face or elsewhere. In a very discreet way, I tried to cover with my hands the most fragile parts of my body, but right before the first pitch, Pastor Perez showed up. Sure enough, I heard the voice. "Jose, our catcher is here, can you sit on the bench for a bit?"

I sat quietly, waiting for one of the pastors to get hurt, or die, or something. I had really wanted to play, but by now, all my enthusiasm was gone. Then I heard the voice of Esteban, the captain of the youth team: "Time out. Pastor Jose, what are you doing?"

"I am sitting," I replied. "What does it look like I'm doing?"

"We need you here!"

I made my way back to the youth team and was asked to play center field and hit fourth. Yeah, cleanup hitter!

Now, guess which team I played with for the rest of my eight and a half years in Greater New York? Yup, you got it right—the youth team! Do you know why? Because we were not created by God to sit on the bench. No one wants to be on a team that does not allow them to play. No one wants to belong to an organization where they are not allowed to contribute.

We were not created to sit in a pew in church, look at the back of somebody else's head, and be fed information that we could get online. God created us— human beings of all ages, languages, and colors—to glorify His name, to serve Him, to love others, and to be engaged with Him in the salvation of others.

Sitting no longer cuts it, nor is it a great indicator of spiritual health in our churches. Dear pastor and church leader, the fact that you have hundreds of people sitting in your church pews does not mean you have a healthy church. Your *sending* capacity (the people active in missional ministry in your church) is a much better indicator of the health of your congregation than your *seating* capacity (the people who simply attend church every week).

Evangelism Action 2—Serve
Multiply through engaging all members in ministry and mission.

From 2015 to 2020, we surveyed and discussed with thousands of pastors, members, and church leaders six actions that could revolutionize mission and evangelism across North America. Eighty-six percent ranked "serve" at 7 or higher on a 1–10 scale. It is important that we, as pastors, and our church members understand that engagement in the mission of the church is not only expected of each one but that it is a matter of spiritual life or death. The fact that someone is not able to preach or teach does not mean she or he cannot reach someone.

Every Adventist member in North America must find his or her spiritual gifts and be given an opportunity to serve in some capacity. The counterproductive tradition that many of us grew up with, which only allowed for veterans in the church to hold ministry posts, needs to be laid to rest for good. I would even suggest putting people to work in our churches before baptism and membership. You would be surprised to see what people are capable of when they realize they belong in your church family; believing and behaving will surely follow.

Compassion initiatives, among others mentioned in the chapters of this section, are a great means of involving people in mission by calling them simply to love others in practical ways as Jesus did. People of all ages can do this without any special training or complex qualifications. Our communities are full of people, both poor and affluent, who need love expressed to them in practical ways. *Compassion* is a very powerful buzzword among millennials and Generation Z. Engaging them through meaningful and sustained projects on behalf of others is not difficult. Helping transform individuals and making communities better are very high on their list of priorities. Also, keep in mind that people engaged in mission work are more likely to stay in your church, including younger generations!

My appeal today: let us give our church members of all ages, languages, and colors across North America an opportunity to play!

Please discuss this evangelism action with your church and plan to make it a reality in your setting.

CHAPTER 4

Engage All Members Through
a Ministry of Compassion

Michael Dauncey and Paulo Macena

Pastor Lovejoy enjoys his pastoral ministry. He pastors a multiple-church district in a rural area. The churches are quite small in attendance, and the pastor busies himself with many duties to keep the churches operating as smoothly as possible. He practices the regular duties of a pastor, such as visitation, Bible studies, and preaching. He also willingly puts the bulletin together, organizes the potlucks, and even mows the church lawn! His members are gracious and praise him with many accolades about the hardworking pastor he is. These compliments go a long way and keep Pastor Lovejoy focused on maintaining all these responsibilities for a long time.

Have you lived this scenario? It may be slightly exaggerated, but perhaps you can relate to it. Often, we as pastors are treated with a high level of respect simply because of the position we hold. After a while, when we start taking on more and more responsibilities, we feel like "Super Pastors," and nothing can slow us down or hinder our efforts. It is true that, in smaller church districts, the pastor needs to be quite versatile and flexible—ready to serve at any time. But is this what God has called us to do? Are we, as leaders, to "do" the ministry of the church?

I (Michael Dauncey) remember experiencing a bit of "Super Pastor" syndrome. It is an easy trap to fall into. Fueled by the flock's positive affirmation, we aim to please people, work harder, and add more to our already overflowing plate of responsibilities. However, I would like to ask a question: Is it possible that we have slipped into bad habits? Is this what God has called His leaders to do?

We can judge our worth by our busyness, and it can become a badge of honor. We become great performers. We want to be liked, and we seek affirmation and validation through our great work ethic. We could eventually adopt the dangerous belief that if we are talented enough and smart enough, the membership will think we are great leaders. However, the undeniable truth is that we have been commissioned *not* to do all the work of the church. We are to train and equip the saints. As Paul instructs us, "So Christ himself gave the apostles, the prophets, the evangelists, the pastors and teachers, to equip his people for works of service, so that the body of Christ may be built up" (Ephesians 4:11, 12, NIV). The work of ministry is too much for just the pastor. How was the work of the church done in the first-century church? Total member involvement.

A strong vision for service

The sixty-four-million-dollar question is this: How can we achieve total member involvement and reach the community? How can we get as many people as possible involved in ministry? I do not claim to have all the answers, but I believe there is a very strong key to this. I believe it is important to keep a strong *vision* before the people. You have probably heard this many times before (because it is true): "Everything rises and falls on leadership." It is crucial for us to lead our people with a vision and a common goal. People want to be led. It is truly amazing to see the inspiration people receive when, by catching a vision, they are challenged to a mission.

When a congregation believes in the board-approved vision of the church, things are going to happen. There will be success when members and church leaders are heading down the "freeway of ministry" in the same direction. With good alignment and all four tires rolling, progress is certain. We will arrive at the destination a lot sooner. This unity of purpose is one of the keys to involving the entire church.

If everyone buys into the direction the church has chosen, involvement in the process is a fun and exciting ride! People become so focused on the mission that there is no time for arguing about small things or being distracted with internal church issues. If we as leaders keep the mission constantly in front of the people, regularly pointing to outreach, community service, and making a difference in our world—doing the things Jesus would do if He were physically on earth—it is amazing how distractions just fall away. Without vision, mission, and a specific purpose, it is harder to engage the people.

Finding the right job in which to serve

When trying to get the membership on board with participating in active ministry, there is value in trying to align their gifts and talents with a ministry with which they resonate. In my local context, we have a larger-than-average Seventh-day Adventist congregation, and making our church function properly takes many volunteers. Because of this, the work of the nominating committee (Ministry Placement Team) is a huge and daunting process that we complete every two years.

As I write this, we are putting together our Ministry Placement Team. I am beginning some prework by asking people whether they will continue serving in their current capacity for the next two years. Even though we are asking for a fairly large commitment from the members, I find that most of them are willing! When people are doing something they are passionate about, it does not seem like work to them. The goal is to align people's talents, skills, and hobbies with a ministry opportunity. When that happens, the assignment or ministry is enjoyable and rewarding to the individual. It is finding the perfect place(s) God has for them in His church.

Engaging through service

I (Paulo Macena) got a phone call a few weeks before Christmas. On the other end of the line was a distressed father. Hearing his trembling voice, I could sense his reluctance to share the real reason for his call. He proceeded to tell me his story: He was sick and was unable to work for the last six months. Life had not been easy, and he was struggling to provide for his family. We were nearing Christmas, and he was worried because he knew he would not be able to buy gifts for his two boys. "Can your church help me to get something for my boys?" he asked.

His request pierced my heart. As a father, I could imagine the pain of being unable to afford even a simple gift for my daughters at Christmas. Without hesitation, I told him that we would help. His kids would not spend Christmas without a present.

At that moment, I started thinking about all the people who, for one reason or another, would be unable to have a very merry Christmas. I thought about single moms who live in shelters or a father who has lost his job and is struggling with unemployment. How difficult would it be for them to buy gifts for their kids during Christmastime? Then a thought came to my mind: *We have a church for goodness sake! We have members coming to church every Sabbath, warming the benches! We can help! We* do *have the resources needed to help.* That year, I challenged the members of my church to be compassionate and serve others during Christmas. In just a couple of days, we collected hundreds of toys for boys and girls of different ages and an abundance of food we could give away.

I clearly remember stopping the van in front of the house of the father who had called me before. He came out with his two boys to meet me. I opened the van's door and told the father to choose whatever he wanted to give to his kids. He gratefully accepted.

Our next stop was at a mothers' shelter, where we visited two single moms. We stepped aside and allowed them, along with their children, to choose whatever they wanted. The moms were excited, and the kids were giggling and laughing. They clung to the toys they chose, and with smiles on their faces, they looked at us with expressions of gratitude.

These two small acts of compassion, alleviating these families' worries, warmed my heart. They would be spending Christmas with dignity, celebrating with their kids. Some of us are fortunate; we have the opportunity to share with others. The reason God blesses our churches is so that we can bless others.

The ripple effect of compassion
In 2 Corinthians 9:8–13, Paul put it this way:

God will generously provide all you need. Then you will always have everything you need and plenty left over to share with others. As the Scriptures say,

"They share freely and give generously to the poor.
Their good deeds will be remembered forever."

For God is the one who provides seed for the farmer and then bread to eat. In the same way, he will provide and increase your resources and then produce a great harvest of generosity in you.

Yes, you will be enriched in every way so that you can always be generous. And when we take your gifts to those who need them, they will thank God. So two good things will result from this ministry of giving—the needs of the believers in Jerusalem will be met, and they will joyfully express their thanks to God.

As a result of your ministry, they will give glory to God. For your generosity to them and to all believers will prove that you are obedient to the Good News of Christ (NLT).

This passage describes the ripple effect of compassion! God provides for us so that we can provide for others. Then, as a result of our ministry of compassion, they will be grateful and will glorify God. Our generosity and service "proves that we are obedient to the Good News of Christ" (verse 13, NLT). Paul reminds us that obedience is not about following a bunch of rules disconnected from humanity; instead, we demonstrate our faithfulness to God by helping others.

Many of the religious leaders in Jesus' time had no problem following rules and commandments, but their obedience was destitute of love for people. Jesus came to show us that our love for God goes beyond mere words. Jesus did not stay in heaven, contemplating humanity's need for salvation and discussing it with His Father. Jesus, the God of the universe, came to earth to *show* compassion. He spoke to people. He healed them. He spread love. He served. He chose to die so we can live. His love was active, not passive.

In the same way, our love for people must be active. Our compassion cannot be passive. If we know what we must do, let us do it! This is not a new idea or a new commandment. Jesus said we must love others, and He gave us an example. He showed us how to love them—through acts of compassion and service.

Read this Bible parable carefully: "Then the King will say to those on His right hand, 'Come, you blessed of My Father, inherit the kingdom prepared for you from the foundation of the world: for you came to church and sang songs from the hymnal, you read from the King James Version, you gave your tithes and offerings, you put out so many fires between members of your church, you kept a vegetarian diet, you wore a suit and tie to look important, you worked for the church, you became a pastor, and once in a while you served someone. Now enter to the kingdom of God.' "

Wait! That is not what the Bible says! However, that is how many people are living their Christian lives. We think that by following a task, a tradition, or just attending a church, we are engaged and already fulfilling Jesus' great commission. Jesus has a different experience in mind. Here is what He said: "Come, you blessed of My Father, inherit the kingdom prepared for you from the foundation of the world: for I was hungry and you gave Me food; I was thirsty and you gave Me drink; I was a stranger and you took Me in; I was naked and you clothed Me; I was sick and you visited Me; I was in prison and you came to Me" (Matthew 25:34–36, NKJV). Do you see the difference?

These are simple acts of compassion that anyone can do. Moreover, getting the members engaged in service *must* start with you, their pastor![1]

Note that Jesus' words were not to a church or an organization but to His disciples. In following Jesus' example, the disciples were not invited to lead from the pulpit; they were expected to go out among the people and serve those in need. The same is expected from each one of us today. As Christ's followers, our "life must be like Christ's life—between the mountain and the multitude."[2] Jesus was on the mountain, praying and seeking God, but then He was with the multitude. The problem is that as leaders, we are teaching our members to climb the mountain to pray and seek God, but we fail to teach them that they must go down and serve the multitude.

How can you serve?

Our church's greatest resource is people—people who come and go week after week. Many of them leave the church frustrated because they feel they are of no help. We often fail to recognize that our members are unique individuals searching for meaning. They come from different backgrounds and different cultures. They have different values and different careers. They walk on different paths of life. Nevertheless, all of them, without exception, have one thing in common: they want to find their purpose here on earth. To engage our members in the ministry of compassion, we simply have to ask, How can you help? It is amazing how things change when you start asking this simple question. You do not need a degree to serve others. You do not need a ton of money. You do not even need approval from the church board! Incredibly, when we ask our members how they can serve, amazing things start to happen. Engagement is inevitable because they feel they are part of something greater than themselves.

Sister White once had a vision of a special church in San Francisco—a church that would serve its community through many different activities. That church became a reality, and a few years later, she went to visit it. This is how she described it:

> During the past few years, the "beehive" in San Francisco has indeed been a busy one. Many lines of Christian effort have been carried forward by our brothers and sisters there. These included visiting the sick and destitute, finding homes for orphans, and work for the unemployed; nursing the sick, and teaching the truth from house to house; the distribution of literature, and the conducting of classes on healthful living and the care

of the sick. A school for the children has been conducted in the basement of the Laguna Street meeting-house. For a time a working men's home and medical mission was maintained. On Market Street, near the city hall, there were treatment rooms, operated as a branch of the St. Helena Sanitarium. In the same locality was a health food store. Nearer the center of the city, not far from the Call building, was conducted a vegetarian café, which was open six days in the week, and entirely closed on the Sabbath. Along the water front, ship mission work was carried on. At various times our ministers conducted meetings in large halls in the city. Thus the warning message was given by many.[3]

What a beautiful church! Indeed, an engaged church that started with a vision! A church that was not only praying and seeking God's presence but also serving the community in many different areas. A church that was using its members' talents and skills to attend to its neighbors' needs. A church that was going up to the "mountain" to seek God but was coming right back down to serve the multitude. We want that church! Having our members involved, encouraged, and engaged in mission starts with a vision, and a vision becomes a reality only when we dare to ask the people of our church a simple question: How can you serve? That is the only way to engage all members and leave no one behind. We must lead them to service—a vibrant, appealing, dynamic ministry of compassion.

---

1. Previously published in Paulo Macena, "Nike Is Right. Just Do It!" NADMinisterial, October 26, 2018, https://www.nadministerial.com/stories/2018/10/26/nike-is-right-just-do-it.

2. Ellen G. White, *Steps to Christ* (Washington, DC: Review and Herald®, 1956), 101.

3. Ellen G. White, "Notes of Travel—No. 3," *Advent Review and Sabbath Herald*, July 5, 1906, 8.

Michael Dauncey has been the lead coordinator for unique community outreach activities, such as Extreme Home Repair, Breakfast Club, Single Mom's Oil Change, and Cars for Moms during the past ten years. He is passionate about matching ministry opportunities with people's spiritual gifts and providing opportunities for them to become active in ministry.

Paulo Macena is the lead pastor for Ellicott City SDA Church and Urban Life Center, a Baltimore Center of Influence, in the Chesapeake Conference. He holds a master of arts in youth ministry and a doctor of ministry in leadership, both from Andrews University. He is also the founder of the Adventist Leadership Institute (adventistleadership.com). Pastor Macena authored The Missing Power, published by the General Conference Ministerial Association.

Acts of Kindness
Video Presentation (RT: 15:48)
Michael Dauncey

How to Engage
Members Into Service
Video Presentation (RT: 18:57)
Paulo Macena

CHAPTER 5

Connect Your Church to the Community for Effective Ministry

Jerome M. Hurst

Collaboration is not just a buzzword these days. It is a necessity for successful ministry in today's world. We live in a world with many challenges, a world in which everyone is looking to see how the church will respond. The truth is, community problems and issues are far too complex for any church, agency, or organization to tackle. It is imperative that the church partner with others in bringing solutions to the issues faced in the communities we serve. "Collaboration is the key that *reduces the duplication* of our efforts, *maximizes the impact* of our ministries, and *strengthens the credibility* of our witness for Christ."[1]

The challenge, of course, is not that people are opposed to partnership in principle. Few people we have ever met would say that Christians should *not* work together. The messages of the Scriptures in support of practical collaboration are clear. Following are just a few:

First Corinthians 12:12, 13: "For example, the body is one unit and yet has many parts. As all the parts form one body, so it is with Christ. By one Spirit we were all baptized into one body. Whether we are Jewish or Greek, slave or free, God gave all of us one Spirit to drink" (GW).

Proverbs 27:17: "As one piece of iron sharpens another, so friends keep each other sharp" (ERV).

Hebrews 10:24, 25: "And let us consider how to stir up one another to love and good works, not neglecting to meet together, as is the habit of some, but encouraging one another, and all the more as you see the Day drawing near" (ESV).

Ecclesiastes 4:9: "Two are better than one, because they have a good reward for their toil" (ESV).

The real challenge is the gap between the stated values and the actual practice of Christian organizations. Unfortunately, many believe that

> interaction betrays their own biblical distinctiveness. I regret that more than a few of my fellow Seventh-day Adventists fall into that exclusivist mindset.
>
> Invariably, [we] quote Ellen G. White in holding [ourselves] aloof from fellowship with the larger Christian community. It's true that Ellen White initially was a separatist who shared the "shut door" mentality of ex-Millerite Sabbatarians. But as she matured in her theology over the years, she extended herself into connectivity with the wider Christian community. . . .
>
> For example, in the 1880s, Ellen White joined forces with the Women's Christian Temperance Union, a group of Protestant prohibitionists. She spoke at their rallies and even recommended that some of our best Adventist talent should work for that organization.[2]

She gave this additional counsel: "The Lord has His representatives in all the churches."[3] "We should unite with other people just as far as we can and not sacrifice principle."[4]

"It should ever be manifest that we are reformers, but not bigots. When our laborers enter a new field, they should seek to become acquainted with the pastors of the several churches in the place. Much has been lost by neglecting to do this. If our ministers show themselves friendly and sociable . . . , it will have an excellent effect, and may give these pastors and their congregations favorable impressions of the truth."[5]

"Light has been given to me that there are those with most precious talents and capabilities in the Women's Christian Temperance Union [W.C.T.U.]. Much time and money have been absorbed among us in ways that bring no returns. Instead of this, some of our best talent should be set at work for the W.C.T.U., *not as evangelists*, but as those who fully appreciate the good that has been done by this body. We should seek to gain the confidence of the workers in the W.C.T.U. by harmonizing with them as far as possible."[6]

I believe that the main reason we have experienced this gap between stated values and actual practice is that most Christian leaders simply do not have the hands-on skills to collaborate. In the remainder of this chapter, I will share, from my personal experience, some tools and techniques that I have used.

Before meeting with those outside our organization, there must be an understanding of self by both the leader and the church. Each leader must confirm God's calling upon his or her life and on the ministry of the church. In order to reach our community, we, as leaders and church, must love the community. We can never reach a community that we do not love. We will never reach people whom we are unwilling to love. We must see those in the community as people whom God loves, and whom Jesus died for, not merely as potential members of our church.

Find your community's needs

After looking at the leader and the church, consider the needs of your city and community. Some needs in your city might be obvious, such as a newspaper headline that shouts, "Local Stabbing Connected to City's Gang Growth." Some needs in your community may only be a whisper, such as staggering numbers of infant mortality or children suffering from lead paint poisoning. In order to connect with the community, the church members must know the community you want to help and the people groups you need to serve.

You can find information about your community by reviewing the statistical data available at the official US Census website, factfinder.census.gov. This website is filled with various levels of reports. You will find more than population data. There is information about social, economic, and housing characteristics. You can also discover data about how many people are out of work due to disability, how many are divorced, or how many people live below the poverty level, and much more. This information will assist you in the development of your outreach ministry.

Beyond the statistical data, I recommend you speak with individuals who live in the community. Be intentional about taking the time to get to know and understand the community and the people whom you are called to reach. There are simple ways to do this:

- *Porch talks.* Go house to house in the community and talk with the residents. You can use a survey to direct the conversation.
- *Block associations or street clubs.* Some communities have groups of people that meet regularly to discuss issues and solutions that pertain specifically to their locale. A representative from the church should hold membership and attend those meetings, and the church could host meetings.
- *Community hot spots.* Go to the places where people from the community hang out, such as barber and beauty shops, coffee shops,

parks, fast-food restaurants, or diners. Just start hanging out with the people and get to know them.

Build relationships

As we continue to gather information about the community, we can also begin to build relationships that could lead to partnerships. Three types of organizations are valuable community partners with whom I believe we should build relationships:

1. *Community-based.* Look to organizations working alongside you on the front lines of your community. Local nonprofits may find that your values fit well with theirs, even if you are offering different types of services.
2. *Government-based.* Local governmental institutions may also be excellent partner organizations to explore. Schools and educational institutions may be excellent partners, and they can provide access to the population your church serves. Statewide partnerships are also important because of their data repositories.
3. *Faith-based.* If their mission aligns with yours, partner with local religious institutions. Places of worship are often regarded as important resources for a community and have diverse congregations with various skills.[7]

There are people in each of these organizations who know more about the community than you. As church leaders, we can learn about our community from other local organizations that care for it. Pick up the phone. Call the organizations and agencies in your area and learn about their mission. Following is a list of the community organizations and agencies to contact:

- Local government officials
- Pastors
- School board members
- Chamber of commerce
- Community service agencies
- School administrators
- Police officers and firefighters
- Hospitals and health-care professionals

Questions can guide the discussion with the community leaders listed above, such as, What are the three best-kept secrets about this community? Who are three people that love this community and understand the people who live here? What changes do you see on the horizon for this community? What are some of the most significant events that have taken place in this community? What is the most difficult part of your job? How may we pray for you? What can the churches of _____ do to make this community better?

Here are some questions you should ask yourselves:

- It has been said that you cannot lead others where you are unwilling to go. Deuteronomy 15:11 says, "There will always be poor people in the land. Therefore I command you to be openhanded toward your fellow Israelites who are poor and needy in your land" (NIV). In what ways are you openhanded?
- Proverbs 31:8, 9 reads, "Speak up for those who cannot speak for themselves, for the rights of all who are destitute" (NIV). Whom are you speaking for?
- What local nonprofit organizations does your church currently support with volunteers and/or donations?
- How could you strengthen or expand those partnerships to learn more about the needs in your city?
- In your church, who is already well-connected in the community by vocation, civic leadership, or volunteering?
- How well are those people connected to the church? How could you leverage their knowledge of the community to strengthen your congregation's ministry to the community?

It takes work to build the relationships necessary to have effective collaboration. Most people will not take the time; thus, they will never truly impact their community. However, some will put in both the time and the effort. My prayer is that this chapter will, at least, light a fire within you to gather more information and *begin* doing something *now*.

A case study

The program Safe Streets/Safe Schools is a collaboration between churches, schools, communities, and government. The principle partners are Connect-Clev, City of Cleveland, Cleveland Public Schools, AmeriCorps, and local churches and community members.

Safe Streets/Safe Schools was developed by five clergy members (which has developed into a collaboration called ConnectClev) in response to the January

2017 murder of Alliana Defreeze, a student at E Prep Elementary School. She was abducted near E. 93rd and Kinsman Road following a bus ride from home toward the school and was later found brutally murdered in an abandoned home in the area.

In response, Safe Streets/Safe Schools was organized to create safe and healthy communities to support students traveling to Cleveland schools in the early hours. As a first step, the participating pastors responded with immediate grief counseling at the school and high-visibility foot patrols before school, offering support and comfort to students.

Along with these steps, the pastors carried out a strategic planning project and engaged in research to develop a sustainable model. The initial model included four actions: (1) identifying adult monitors to patrol around the school, (2) encouraging students to walk or travel to and from school in groups, (3) distributing information and tool kits on school and community safety and school-based bullying, and (4) working with parents and residents engaging in advocacy to address blight, abandoned buildings, and infrastructure issues, such as weak and crumbling sidewalks.

The project took shape with notable positive outcomes and was maintained for the remainder of that school year (January 2017 to May 2017) without interruption or grant funds. Activities during the period also included planning and training with both the City of Cleveland/CMSD Safe Routes to School Program and the City of Cleveland Department for Prevention, Intervention, and Opportunity for Youth and Young Adults.

In August 2018, ConnectClev received continuation funding from the City of Cleveland to implement an expanded framework for Safe Streets/Safe Schools. Based on feedback from parents and residents, the expanded model incorporated employment and financial literacy–based programming into the overall framework. The Safe Streets/Safe Schools theory of change states, "Children are inherently safer when they come from families and communities that are financially stable." Safe Streets/Safe Schools continues to serve four of the five original schools/communities and envisions becoming a citywide initiative.

The program has several key components:

- *Hiring and training a site coordinator for the four hub churches.* The site coordinator is responsible for developing "opportunity centers," which serve as "one-stop service hubs" linked to the target schools and the City of Cleveland recreation centers. Each "opportunity center" provides services such as financial literacy, job readiness, a food pantry, and support groups. They may also provide additional services that are unique to the church or community they serve.

- *Recruiting community neighborhood residents (parents and additional faith leaders) to serve as street monitors.* This recruitment incorporates members of the community and other churches into the program.
- *Training student safety ambassadors.* These students (two per school) lead our "walking school bus" initiative. This initiative is the centerpiece of the nationally recognized Safe Routes to School Program. It is designed to inspire and equip students to walk as a team to and from school under the theme "no child walks alone."
- *Offering school-based workshops.* The workshops were on subjects such as school safety, community crime, bullying, attendance/academic success, and safe-summer tool kits.

The churches and school associations are as follows: A. J. Rickoff, Zion Hill Baptist Church; R. H. Jamison, Southeast Seventh-day Adventist Church; Mound, Fountain of Grace; Miles Park, Greater Love Baptist Church.

While our program is school-based, we have attempted to follow the students and parents into the community. Our plan for the "opportunity centers" is to connect with parents and students during after-school hours and to reach parents who may work during the day. Our overall engagement strategy is based on referrals from city recreation centers. We have identified several key partners, which we use for the core services.

Through collaborative efforts with the City of Cleveland recreation centers, Safe Streets/Safe Schools circles will serve as a catalyst to engage individuals and families in geographically defined areas to achieve personal goals and objectives. Safe Streets/Safe Schools strives to develop healthy and resilient communities and families through its relationship with each school.

1. Kärin Butler Primuth, "How Networks Are Shaping the Future of World Mission," *Mission Frontiers*, March–April 2017, http://www.missionfrontiers.org/issue/article/how-networks-are-shaping-the-future-of-world-mission; emphasis added.

2. Martin Weber, " 'How Adventists Are Blessed by Other Christians,' " The Story Church Project (blog), https://thestorychurchproject.com/bloghost/tag/Christians.

3. Ellen G. White, *Testimonies for the Church*, vol. 6 (Mountain View, CA: Pacific Press®, 1948), 70.

4. H. M. Kenyon, "Michigan Health and Temperance Association," *Advent Review and Sabbath Herald*, October 21, 1884, 14.

5. Ellen G. White, "Overcoming Prejudice," *Advent Review and Sabbath Herald*, June 13, 1912, 3.

6. Ellen G. White, Manuscript 91, 1907; emphasis added.

7. John Snow, Inc., *Engaging Your Community: A Toolkit for Partnership, Collaboration, and Action*, January 2012, 8, https://publications.jsi.com/JSIInternet/Inc/Common/_download_pub.cfm?id=14333&lid=3.

Jerome Hurst is the senior pastor of the Ethnan Temple Seventh-day Adventist Church in Wilkinsburg, Pennsylvania, and the Community Service and Public Affairs and Religious Liberties director for the Allegheny West Conference. In recognition of his deep involvement in community-based ministry, Hurst was inducted into the Dr. Martin Luther King Jr. Board of Preachers at Morehouse College and was also elected to serve as first vice president for the Cleveland Chapter of the NAACP.

**Building Bridges,
Tearing Down Walls**
Video Presentation (RT: 20:01)
Jerome Hurst

CHAPTER 6

Trusting and Releasing Volunteer Lay Pastors for Mission

Patty Crouch

Rock bottom! The Perry church had hit rock bottom with, what seemed like, nowhere to go from there. The Florida Conference thought long and hard and concluded that the best thing for the church would be to close it down and have the few members who were attending church in Perry travel an hour away to one of our sister churches. The Perry church was a small block building about sixty years old located just a few feet from the railroad tracks. The train would come by every Sabbath morning during worship service, rattling the building and blowing the whistle so loud that the speakers would have to stop speaking or try to shout over the train. The church needed many repairs. It had ten small pews able to seat only about thirty to forty comfortably.

The location and condition of the building, however, were not the main reason the church was at the point of no return. The cracks in the foundation of the building were nothing compared to the cracks in the foundation of the people—not all of them, just a handful. But that is all it takes in a small church in a small town. That is all it takes in any church in any town. The church had a reputation in the community of self-righteousness, and the members were known as the Saturday worshipers, worshipers of a day, not worshipers of the Lord. They were known as the people who do not eat pork or go out on Friday night and, sadly, were even known for racism. Again, not all the members were this way. Nevertheless, a handful of members with judgmental, self-righteous, racist hearts is all that it takes to kill a church.

My husband, Brian, our two sons, and I moved to Perry, Florida, from Michigan. Being outsiders, not brought up in the Perry church, we can tell you that, unfortunately, the view that the community had of the church was true. Even if the entire church died out, left, or even had a change of heart, the community would always relate that building with the people of the past. We watched this little church go through many ups and downs, struggling just to survive. We watched as good pastors came and went, never staying longer than they had to.

Through those years and struggles, I worked with the youth, trying to keep them encouraged and involved with the church and community, trying to provide a safe environment for them to grow and be themselves. I longed for our church to be a place of unconditional love. It was not. The time had come. Another good pastor and his family left. The good ones always did. This time, when the conference visited us, it was not to assign us a new pastor. They told us that we did not qualify for a new pastor and that our elders could speak until they could find us a volunteer lay pastor.

In a few months, they found someone willing to drive an hour and a half to come to preach on Sabbath morning. Things seemed to be going well. Then, the unthinkable happened. He passed away unexpectedly from an aneurysm. So there we were again, struggling, only a handful attending, and without a pastor.

Again came the visit from the conference—this time with the recommendation of closing the church as our best option. No volunteer lay pastors lived within driving distance, and we could not have either a full-time or part-time paid pastor. They decided to give us one more chance and sent Elder Bob Bogus to our church to evaluate the situation and help find a possible solution. After several meetings and lots of prayer, Elder Bogus asked me to become a volunteer lay pastor. I thought he was crazy! I did not fit in as it was, and I was a woman. Those were two strikes against me already. He replied that he had prayed about it, and the Holy Spirit had told him to ask me. He asked me to take a leap of faith and trust that the Holy Spirit would lead. After fervent prayer, I fearfully and reluctantly said yes.

I enrolled in the Volunteer Lay Pastor program and began the journey of leading the church. This solution did not make some folks very happy, and the declining church's average attendance of eight or ten became even less. Some believed that if you are a volunteer, you are not a real pastor, and if you are a woman, that is even worse. A volunteer woman leading the church is blasphemy!

People leaving the church is not always a bad thing; some people need to get out of the way so that the Holy Spirit can take control. I also figured, what have we got to lose? We are already at rock bottom. *This is sink-or-swim time*, I thought, *so if we are going down, we may as well go down fighting*. This time, however, I was determined that the fight was not going to be squabbling between members as usual. This time, the battle belonged to the Lord.

We began to pray and seek God's presence, asking Him to transform our hearts, change our attitudes, and forgive us for failing Him, for failing our mission, and for failing each other. We also prayed for God to help us become the church He had called us to be. You see, there is no sense in trying to evangelize and bring people into a camp of infected soldiers—infected with self, with indifference, racism, hate, pride, and the like. The infection will just spread throughout the camp.

After months of praying together and drawing closer to each other and to the Lord, we began developing a genuine love for one another. It was not that "I love you because I am a Christian and I have to love you" fake kind of love, but a genuine love—the John 15:13 kind of love. "Greater love has no one than this, than to lay down one's life for his friends" (NKJV). Now we were ready to reach out to our community and to offer them love and give them Jesus.

The church had held failed evangelistic meetings several times in the past, but we decided to try it one more time—this time with a whole new attitude. We were now looking to reach souls for heaven, not looking to add numbers to the church. We were motivated by love, not religion.

When the evangelist and his wife arrived, looked over the place, and learned about our church's history, they suggested that we should not hold the meetings at the church. So we held them in an old house that belonged to the church and that we were currently using for youth activities and events on Saturday nights. That was it—the perfect opportunity to continue breaking the chains that were holding us back. I knew we needed to leave that old block building and its reputation behind. The few of us who were left agreed it was time to put that building up for sale and continue our worship services in the house with plans of one day building a church. At the beginning of the meetings, we had an average of eight to ten members attending. At the end of the meetings, we had baptized eight people, and four came in by profession of faith. Now that may seem like small numbers, but it was double what we started with, and others were still to come.

We sold the building on the tracks and began raising funds for a new church building, all the while doing whatever we could just to love people and give them Jesus. A few of the practical ways we loved people to Jesus were by simply meeting their needs. For single mothers or families that were struggling to make ends meet, we provided free childcare, diapers, food, school supplies, and birthday parties. We took teens to Christian concerts and took them shopping, allowing them to pick out their own school clothes. We had movie nights, bowling nights, and camp meetings at Kulaqua, and, did I mention, we loved them? We provided free marriage counseling for couples. We took the elderly grocery shopping, or we shopped for them if they were not up to it. We had open mic night with games, activities, bonfires, and cookouts. Music and food on Saturday evenings was a favorite time for young and not so young, alike.

Everyone was invited and encouraged to participate in the evening worship service in whatever way they felt led, members and nonmembers, singing, playing instruments, dramas, poetry, and comedy. Children, from the time they could walk and talk, were encouraged to participate, preparing them to be our leaders.

Our church today is a place where people come together. At one time, the rooms were separated by generations who were anxious for the services to end. Today, members and visitors of all ages enjoy worship and fellowship together, and they all come back in the evening for more. Our church is a place that welcomes, loves, and encourages the ones who were once condemned for what they were wearing to participate in worship exactly as they are, whether they are wearing jeans and a T-shirt or a suit and tie.

Jesus did not die for the suit and tie

We sold the old building, left the old reputation behind. With much work, fundraising, donations, blood, sweat, tears, and the help of Maranatha volunteers and some volunteers from a few of our sister churches, we built a new church building. Since this new church was built, more than thirty souls have been baptized or have recommitted their lives to Jesus! And this is just the beginning.

Serving the Lord as a volunteer lay pastor (VLP) has been one of the most humbling, rewarding, exciting, fun, and at times, heartbreaking, frustrating, and exhausting missions I have ever been on. At the beginning of this journey, I was told by a member of the church that if I took the VLP position, the church would go down the drain, that we would not even be able to pay our electric bills, and that we would have to close down our church. I was told to decline the VLP position and to encourage everyone to stop paying tithes so we would force the conference to give us a real pastor. Numerous times, both members and leaders of the Adventist Church have asked questions like, "When will the Perry church get a real pastor?" "Don't you realize it is not biblical for women to lead or pastor a church?" I have been informed by fellow

Adventists that VLPs are just a way for our conferences to get out of paying pastors and that VLPs would not be as dedicated to the church. Folks who call themselves Christians have condemned and ridiculed me just for being a woman who accepted a calling to serve the Lord.

On the other hand, I have also been encouraged and supported by leaders, pastors, and members throughout the NAD and the VLP program. I have been prayed with and prayed for, with continual training and equipping to take on the responsibility of leading in a church. I have also been given opportunities to renew and refresh with other VLPs. I have had the privilege of baptizing beautiful souls from the age of ten to the mid-eighties, including my father. He was there when I was born, and I was there when he was re-born; that alone was worth all the condemnation and criticism I have received throughout this journey. I have also had the opportunity to witness God heal marriages and diseases, deliver people from addictions and from self, pride, prejudice, and hate. Moreover, I had the privilege to witness God raising the dead—our church—and transforming it into a living church that is driven and motivated by love. A church that was once ready to breathe its last breath is now replanted, reborn, and rooted in love through the power of the Holy Spirit and a little assistance from a female VLP.

I have learned a few things along the way:

- People say that we are not all called to do the same thing. I disagree. We are all called to love! To love God and to love people. We have all merely been given different gifts and talents to accomplish this calling.
- Several people have stated that VLPs are here to take jobs from full-time pastors. The truth is that volunteer lay pastors are not here to take the jobs of full-time pastors. On the contrary, we are here to help lift the burden and lighten the load for our full-time pastors. We do not compete with full-time pastors; we partner with them.
- Another rumor is that VLPs will not be as dedicated because they are volunteers. VLPs are just as devoted as full-time pastors are. Many of the VLPs lead successful and thriving churches while working at full-time jobs.
- Yet another rumor is women should not be pastors or VLPs because they are too weak to be leaders, and it is not biblical. I am not going into the heated debate of women pastors. However, the truth is, there are thriving, successful churches led by strong female VLPs and strong female pastors across the North American Division of Seventh-day

Adventists. Some of the most hurtful words have been spoken to me, and about me, by fellow Adventists. They were spoken just because I am a woman who said yes to God's calling to lead a divided, declining church from closing its doors to becoming a thriving church family, united in love, and with a passion for loving others to Jesus.

I have been in rooms with people who smoke and people who are self-righteous and racist, and I will take my chances with secondhand smoke any day; it is less intrusive. People must be more important to us than our opinions, music style, dress codes, political views, and human-made traditions. No matter what your past is, how bad or good you have been, how educated you are, whether you have a college education or not, whether you are a boy, girl, man, or woman; the Holy Spirit of God can, and will, use you to lead others to the foot of the cross because, with Him, all things really are possible.

Conversation starter questions

1. Is it harder for a congregation to trust a VLP with the responsibility of leading a church versus a full-time pastor? Why or why not?
2. Do racism and prejudice exist in our churches and within our leaders today? If so, what are we to do about it?
3. Is there a time to close the doors of a church and call it quits? Why or why not?

Patty Crouch has been in youth ministry for more than fifteen years. While serving as youth director at the Perry Seventh-day Adventist Church in Florida, she also served as a volunteer lay pastor, and a second church was planted. During her ministry at the Perry Church, the youth group grew from an average attendance of between eight and ten to between thirty and forty with thirty to fifty or more in attendance at the Saturday night activities.

Reflect Love
Video Presentation (RT: 19:26)
Patty Crouch

ACTION 3—BAPTIZE

Multiply through providing many opportunities for people to commit to Jesus and the church.

It Should Not Be an Option

Jose Cortes Jr.

And the Lord added to the church daily those who were being saved.
—Acts 2:47, NKJV

There is no substitute for proclamation! If we want people to learn about Jesus' love and His grace offered freely to each one of us sinners, we must not only show them with our actions but also tell them with our words. If we want people to understand the plan of redemption and Jesus' command to love others, as well as the hope of His second coming and the resurrection of those who have followed Him, we must tell them. If we really want them to live healthier lives and take time out to worship and rest on the Sabbath, we must let them know.

Neither is there a substitute for inviting people to accept Jesus and join the body of Christ, the church, through baptism. If we want people to accept Jesus as Savior and Lord, publicly commit to Him through baptism, and join the church, we have to be willing to invite those who have not yet made a decision.

If we preach awesome sermons and no one is accepting Jesus, being baptized, and joining the church as a result of our preaching, perhaps we are just giving speeches. If we produce amazing church programs while decisions for Jesus and the church are not being made as a result of those programs, perhaps we are just putting up a mission-less religious display. The reason Jesus came to this earth, died, founded the church, and asked us to proclaim the gospel is that people would accept Him, be baptized, and be saved. If we are not providing opportunities for this to take place regularly through our churches, we may not be doing Jesus, the church, our programs, and our preaching any justice.

Evangelism Action 3—Baptize
Multiply through providing many opportunities for people to commit to Jesus and the church.

From 2015 to 2020, we surveyed and discussed with thousands of pastors, members, and church leaders six actions that could revolutionize mission and evangelism across North America. Seventy-seven percent ranked "baptize" at 7 or higher on a 1–10 scale. As the church of God that has been trusted with such a life-transforming gospel, we cannot afford to neglect inviting people on a regular and constant basis to accept our Savior and join our church.

The good news must be imparted by some means. Everybody ought to know. Therefore, I would encourage every pastor and able lay leader in North America to find many different and tactful ways to constantly keep the invitation before those who have not made a decision.

When it comes to proclamation evangelism, one way or one size does not fit all. Perhaps this is one of the reasons why proclamation evangelism has become so burdensome for some; we feel we must do what others have done and have the same success they have had. It is OK to apply principles that work; yet, you are not obligated to follow a school that does not apply to your context.

You do not have to fight the giant in King Saul's armor. Please find something that works in your context and put it into practice. I know churches that use their funding to bless the community through incarnational evangelism and make every Sabbath an evangelistic service, with the needs of the unchurched in mind. I know pastors who have successfully used a CrossFit gym for a week to present the gospel to health enthusiasts. I know families who invite their friends and neighbors to a smaller gathering in the privacy of their homes and present the gospel in a very informal way that is effective. Social media proclamation has also been used effectively by several pastors in North America.

As a corporate church, we must give organizational permission and flexibility to pastors and church members to create effective templates for the proclamation of the gospel—a proclamation that tells the story, allows people to know about Jesus, gives them the opportunity to accept Him as Savior and Lord, and provides space for them to become a part of the body of Christ. If something does not work, take note of it, make changes, and try again. It is OK to try different methods and issue different types of invitations and appeals. What is not OK is to spend a whole year preaching and holding church services and programs without giving people opportunities to accept Jesus, be baptized, and join the church. Not inviting people to make a decision and join should not be an option for Adventist pastors, preachers, volunteer lay pastors, nor churches in North America.

Please, discuss this evangelism action with your church and how to make it a reality to reach people who have not made a decision for Jesus and for the Adventist church in your community.

CHAPTER 7

Repeat the Proclamation Evangelism Cycle

Roger Hernández

Like having a baby

One of the concerns I most often hear from pastors is summarized in what someone once told me: "I had an evangelistic series. We baptized twenty-five. Of those, one still comes to church—infrequently." This outcome happens often enough to make me pause and wonder.

As I see it, we have two options before us:

1. We stop doing public evangelism because it is, obviously, the problem.
2. We understand that evangelism is not the problem, but the way we do it can be.

I am going to be pretty blunt. I hope you listen to what I am saying and what I am not saying. In more than twenty-five years, I have had multiple conversations and personal experiences as a pastor and as a pastor's pastor. I usually do a minimum of six evangelistic campaigns per year. I am very concerned about bringing in new members. I am also very concerned about keeping them in. As we look around North America, the prognosis for the church can seem bleak. "According to the *Churchless* data, in the 1990s, 30% of the American population was unchurched. Today, two decades later, that percentage has risen to more than four in 10 Americans (43%)."[1]

Across all denominations, millions of people who used to attend church have stopped. Ours is no exception. Are many still being baptized? Sure. Do many disconnect after choosing to do so? Regretfully, yes. Nonetheless, I believe we can do better. We must do better. It all starts with examining a familiar entry point of many into our church. It is called evangelism.

Evangelism is like having a baby. If you want to have a healthy baby, three things must happen: (1) conception, (2) pregnancy, and (3) delivery. If you want to produce healthy spiritual babies, the process is seldom completed in one month. There must be an initial connection, a time of gestation, and a smooth delivery done by a person who is more interested in delivering a healthy baby than he is in winning the MBD (most babies delivered) award.

My personal experience in the process of evangelism in a significant amount of North American churches goes something like this: We make no friends with unbelievers. We schedule an evangelistic series—still no friends or Bible studies. We wait for three weeks before the meeting to have the mail carrier do what we should be doing—still, no friends. We start the meeting with the sporadic support of the church members. People come for a month or less, wonder why the church members are not there, accept Bible truths, and get baptized. Still, no friends. A short while later, some leave. Sometimes more than a few. We blame the evangelist or the devil. We blame the new people for not being diligent enough to overcome in one month what has taken us a lifetime to conquer. We rinse and repeat. Let me tell you, having conception, pregnancy, and delivery in one month is called a miscarriage!

If you are concerned about the empty pews that used to be filled, I have encouraging words for you. In this chapter, I will share the evangelism model I have used. It is not original. However, it increases the retention rate by 30 to 40 percent, and it works across racial and demographic lines.

The result of evangelism

Before we get to the cycle of evangelism, let us address the elephant in the room. Why do people leave?

Here are the common answers:

- Some leave because they stopped believing in God.
- Some leave because they stopped believing in some or all of the fundamental beliefs.
- Many leave because of conflicts, disconnection, and personal struggles.

While the following quote might not be true in every case, it certainly applies to many of the people who have stopped attending church: "Behind every heresy, there is a hurt." Our data shows a disturbing trend: "Veteran Adventist Church researcher Monte Sahlin said the reasons people drop out of church often have less to do with what the church does and its doctrines than with problems people experience in their personal lives—marital conflict or unemployment, for example."[2] If we are looking for disciples who make disciples, we need to start seeing evangelism more as a cycle and less as *only* an event.

One small but essential key

You have probably heard that in order to stay connected to the church, most people need at least six friends. Most do not have even one—hence the exodus. (Great name for a Bible book. Not that great for an ecclesiastical reality.) So what are we going to do about it? As part of the cycle of evangelism, I ask you to consider the following suggestions.

1. *Celebration.* Every baptism must be celebrated. Only the devil and like-minded individuals get upset when a prodigal comes back home. Since the best reclaiming strategy is to keep the ones we have, I encourage you to do this:
   a. Make a video recording of the testimony to be shown at the baptism. It will remind the new member in the days to come why he or she made the decision.
   b. Give video and pictures of the baptism itself to the new member.
   c. Provide a banquet for new believers. It can happen quarterly or whenever there is a baptism. If there is joy in heaven, let us join the angels in rejoicing!
2. *Community.* We grow better in a community. Note the older brother's attitude in contrast with the father's in the parable of the prodigal son. One ignored and resented. The other celebrated and embraced. Why not try the following?
   a. Assign a healthy Christian to mentor the new believer. One of the most damaging things that can happen to a new believer is to be blasted with unbalanced materials as they begin their Christian walk.
   b. Provide a new-believer class. New believers should be in a class prepared for them for at least six months after baptism. The ideal time is a year. Ground them in Christ. Teach them righteousness by faith. Teach them how to share their faith. Help them know why they believe.
   c. Visit them at least monthly for the first six months. It is like a marriage. If it passes the first six months without either person

quitting, the probability of the couple staying together increases.

3. *Connection.* I did an evangelistic series in a church in Memphis, Tennessee, and baptized twenty-five people. The board voted that every single one of them was to be involved in some sort of ministry. Some were assigned to be deacons, others to prison ministries, some were given responsibility in small-group leadership or the children's department (after a background check). When new soldiers come to the battlefield, we do not tell them to sit down for a while; we give them a weapon and let them join in. They do not become generals overnight, but telling them to sit on the side of the road and watch others fight can be detrimental to their well-being. Do this:

   a. Assign new believers to a specific, gift-based responsibility.
   b. If your church has small groups, have them join one. Make sure the leader visits them.
   c. One of the first things a new believer should do is be involved in an evangelistic event—a series, a Revelation seminar, or an outreach event. New people have more unchurched friends with whom they can share their faith. Do not miss that opportunity.

4. *Church.* If someone ends up leaving and you want to bring them back, to what are you bringing them back? Is the church ready to receive the prodigals? Churches tend to drift inwardly. It is like walking on a treadmill. If you are not intentional about moving forward, you go backward. There is no standing still. Everything your church does right now is either moving you closer to your goal or keeping you from it.

The three *s*'s

The cycle of evangelism involves three *s*'s:

1. *Stop.* Often the problem is not that the church members are not friendly. The problem is that we are friendly with ourselves. We have good friends to whom we gravitate, sit next to in worship, talk to at the end, and invite over after church. Stop being friendly with only your friends.
2. *Start.* Intentionally look for new people. Engage them in conversation. Sit next to them, introduce yourself, and welcome them. Maybe you are not on the hospitality committee, but do it anyway. The effect when people greet, smile, and welcome a person is amazing. Even if you do not become BFFs, they will leave with a positive impression.

3. *Say.* Say the new person's name. Learn it and say it. Nothing deflates a new member more than to be asked if he is a visitor a year after he got baptized. Look past the jewelry and makeup, or whatever, and see the person. Create such a positive experience for new believers that, even if they leave, their memories of the Father's house are so overwhelmingly positive that they will have no choice but to return.

I know a church in the western United States that has about ninety members. They have been at ninety members for twenty years, but they baptize people every year! Something is not right—that math does not add up! When I inquired as to why, the reason became obvious pretty quickly. Let me explain.

The church started a food bank. Wednesday-night prayer meeting tripled because guests were coming for the food and staying for the service. Several people in the church complained. They said things like, "Who are these new people? Who invited them? They will not take good care of God's house." The pastor started a Christmas tradition of providing a banquet for the community. More than a hundred guests came. In the third year, the board sat him down and said, "Pastor, for the last two years, you have done a Christmas banquet for the community. When are you going to do one for us?" One of the newcomers offered to start a community choir to sing Christmas carols. He was a professional choir director in his country. The response from the music leader in the church was, "That is bringing strange fire into the house of God. He is not Adventist." Sound familiar? I wish this were an isolated incident. It is not.

I am asking you to take an honest look at your church and remind yourself and your people of the reason your church exists. New people stay, or return, to healthy churches. Remind yourself, at least once a day, that your job is not to coddle the ninety-nine, to be satisfied with the nine, or to be content because, at least, one of the sons is still home. Lost people matter to God. Do they matter to you?

A template for a cycle of evangelism
The following template for a cycle of evangelism ends in a weeklong reaping series.

Vision:

1. Present Bible truth in a way that makes sense and that helps believers think and thinkers believe.

2. Train members so that they see service and evangelism as a way of life, not an event.

Preparation • Proclamation • Preservation

1. Nine months before—plan (preparation)

- Meet with your church leaders to present the plan.
- Hold a rally for launching the preparation, proclamation, preservation (PPP) plan to the church.
- Provide all of the members a calendar with all of the important dates that will make up the PPP plan.
- Lock in a location.

2. Eight months before—train (preparation)

- Monthly training begins, preparing the members to get involved in reaching those God misses the most. You can use guest speakers as long as you ask them not merely to speak on a specific topic but also to have the members apply it in practical ways using a hands-on method.
- In order to make the most of the training, pastors incorporate what has been taught into the life of the church and begin putting it into practice as the evangelistic series approaches.
- Sample training topics include the following:

Topic	Category
○ Intercessory Prayer	Preparation
○ Preparing for the Harvest	Preparation
○ Community Bible Studies	Preparation/Preservation
○ Helping People Cross the Line	Proclamation
○ Service Evangelism	Preparation/Preservation
○ Innovative Evangelism	Proclamation/Preservation
○ How to Keep Our Members	Preservation

3. Six months before—small groups (preparation/proclamation)

- Begin building relationships with the people in your communities through community Bible studies.
- Church chooses the small-group curriculum that works best for their church and small groups.
- Encourage your churches to begin a child and youth baptismal class in preparation for the meetings.

4. Four months before—season of service (preparation/proclamation)

- Season of service (SOS) is a forty-day service initiative that seeks to demonstrate God's love in practical ways to the city. It can be described in three words: intentional, impact, involve.
- The plan has three simple steps:

  i. A daily service activity that any person can do. This activity is encouraged in the daily devotional called *Season of Service*. (For more information, email pastorvha@aol.com.)
  ii. An intensive weekend service activity with multiple opportunities to serve as churches, groups, families, and individuals. This activity usually happens around day twenty of the forty days.

     - We will provide the brochures with all SOS weekend opportunities, along with a website where they can sign up to volunteer: www.mycitysos.com.
     - We also provide T-shirts for all those who volunteer.
     - The first round of advertisements for the evangelistic series begins this weekend.

  iii. A Sabbath celebration of service in local churches or all together, where we affirm and thank volunteers for their service at the end of the forty days. We invite and pray for civic leaders and local service organizations at that time. By this time, have the handbills ready for everyone to begin handing out.

5. Three months before—Bible workers arrive (preparation)

- Bible workers can be a blessing to your meetings.

6. Forty days before—God's City, My City—prayer, sharing campaign, and small groups (preparation/proclamation)

- God's City, My City (GCMC) has three components:

    i. Six small-group lessons found in the first part of the book *God's City, My City.* (To order copies, email pastorvha@aol.com.) One lesson for each week, which will lead up to the week of the evangelistic series. These lessons encourage members of the small groups to love the city, pray for the city, engage the city, serve the city, invite the city, transform the city.

        - Free video. For the small group leader or pastor, the video gives a short version of how to teach each lesson. Watch it at https://www.youtube.com/user/pastorRogerHernandez /videos.
        - Free small-group leader training manual. A simple how-to guide for the small group leader. Download it from http://www.slideshare.net/RogerHernandez6/my -citygods-cityhowto.

    ii. "40-Day Prayer and Sharing Devotional" that is in the back of the book *God's City, My City.* We encourage everyone to be praying for each aspect of the evangelistic series and to share their faith daily. The devotional provides several activities:

        - A memory verse to ground them in God's Word
        - Applications to teach them God's Word
        - A practical assignment to put God's Word into action in their life
        - A prayer phone line where people call in and have daily devotionals and pray together as a city

    iii. Sermon series with the same six titles as the small-group lessons, to be developed by the pastor and preached concurrently with the small-group series.

7. Forty days before—advertising and preregistration (preparation)

- Blanket your neighborhood with handbills and posters, radio and newspaper ads, and other promotional material.
- Begin to preregister everyone, including members. Why everyone? To make sure our guests will not feel as if we are singling them out. To create a spirit of fellowship where everyone knows their names. To keep a better record of attendance. To gain a greater sense of commitment among those who are preregistered.

8. Two to three weeks before—volunteer training day (preparation)

- Form committees and assign directors.
- Give each committee director the opportunity to meet their volunteers and go over details and their responsibilities during the week of the series.

Training is an important factor for the organization and the excellence of each area of the series.

Sample of our nightly program

Church Responsible	[church name]	
Time	**Activity**	**Person Responsible**
6:40 P.M.	Movie	A/V Team
7:00 P.M.	Song service (one song + theme song)	
7:10 P.M.	Welcome and prayer/Dismiss children	
7:15 P.M.	Health segment	
7:22 P.M.	Prayer/offering (instrumental music)	
7:25 P.M.	Special music	Guest singer
7:30 P.M.	Message	
8:15 P.M.	Special music/altar call Baptism (music/song) Big gift	
8:30 P.M.	Farewell (music)	

Presentations

Date	Sermon	Description	Adventist Connection
Saturday P.M.	We All Have Issues . . .	Let's be real for a moment. We all have problems. We will study three of the most common problems you and I have and how God's grace impacts them in a positive way. An invitation to be *real*.	Grace
Sunday	Epic Fail	Failure can be your teacher, but it doesn't have to define you. Understand the reasons, opportunities, and reactions to failure. God can help you here and now. An invitation to *victory*.	Great controversy
Monday	Rest	Rather than being just another rat in the rat race, discover the secret to balance. God wants you to Stop. Worship. Rest. An invitation to *balance*.	Sabbath
Tuesday	Dollars and Sense	Someone said we spend money we don't have on things we don't need to impress people we don't even like. Come and understand our part, the perils, and the purpose of money. An invitation to *prosper*.	Finances

Wednesday	Building Bridges	Because sometimes you and your kin can't. Come and learn the three characteristics of a successful family. There will be something for everyone—couples, children, and singles. An invitation to *belong*.	Family
Thursday	My Body, God's House	God cares about what's in your body, what's on your body, and what others do to your body. An invitation to *health*.	Health, healing, heaven
Friday	Beyond the Grave	So far, the ratio of people being born and dying is one to one. We try to avoid thinking and talking about it, but it's coming. Come and learn what happens after you die and why it's important. An invitation to *live*.	State of the dead
Saturday P.M.	Hope Wins!	Hope is not a political slogan or a pipe dream. Hope is what sustains, inspires, and propels. God doesn't consult your past to build your future. An invitation to *decide*.	Baptism

Since the people will have been studying the doctrines in their homes for the previous six months, the sermons are decision sermons while addressing the main beliefs. If you want a copy of the messages, email me, and I will be glad to send them.

Final thought

Whatever you do, do not lose the sense of urgency to share Jesus and His truth far and wide. I invite you to give birth to many new babies this and every year.

---

1. "George Barna & David Kinnaman on the Rise of the Churchless," Barna Group, January 8, 2015, https://www.barna.org/barna-update/culture/702-george-barna-david-kinnaman-on -the-rise-of-the-churchless.

2. Ansel Oliver, "At First Retention Summit, Leaders Look at Reality of Church Exodus," Adventist News Network, November 19, 2013, https://adventist.news/en/news/at-first -retention-summit-leaders-look-at-reality-of-church-exodus/.

Roger Hernandez is the Ministerial and Evangelism director for the Southern Union and holds a master of divinity from Andrews University. He is a prolific writer, authoring more than fourteen books including the Sharing Book of the Year—twice, and the Discipleship Book of the Year, Everyone Welcome. He is a practical and engaging speaker on leadership, evangelism, accountability, and diversity (LEAD).

Evangelism: The Story of Mr. G
Video Presentation (RT: 20:09)
Roger Hernandez

CHAPTER 8

Minister Through the Word and Community Presence

Dustin Hall

I will never forget it. I was about to knock on the door of my next Bible study contact, and the Holy Spirit stopped me in my tracks. I heard Him say, "Dustin, you are about to make vegetarian cocaine addicts." In fact, the study that I held in my hands was on health, specifically clean and unclean foods.

All of my training and traditional Adventist upbringing told me to go through the series of Bible studies as written and make appeals at the end of each study. Right then and there, I realized that I was not studying with this couple because I understood and had concern for them as people. I was studying with them so that they could grasp necessary information, and by accepting this information, they would be one step closer to my desired outcome, baptism. I was at a loss to help them with their real need because the information contained in this study was as far as my understanding of the three angels' messages went. Sure, I could show them that drug use was wrong, but they were strung out. They needed something more transformative than just information. I knew of this couple's drug problem, but I had no idea how to connect the truths I believed with their situation. I did not know how to put the gospel in it. This was the first time that I realized that I was teaching people things that were true, but I was not guiding them to the Way, the Truth, and the Life.

Over the next several years, God led me through a process of learning and maturity. I concluded that, traditionally, we as Seventh-day Adventists have done a great job of telling people *about* the great controversy, but we have done a stunningly poor job of helping people live through it.

The moment of complete clarity for me came as I was driving to the bedside of a young, special-needs girl who was dying from pneumonia in the ICU. I was intimidated because I was a pastor (pastors are supposed to have all the answers), and not just a pastor but a Seventh-day Adventist pastor (the people of the answers). However, in this case, I had no answers for this family. What could I possibly say? When I got to her bedside, I was at a loss; I did not have the words, or the prayers, or the right Bible verses to read. All I could do was stand there with her parents and try to hold back the tears. I did manage to spit out something of an attempt at comfort and prayer and a verse or two. After she passed away and the funeral had ended, the family did not thank me for my kind words or my prayers. In tears, they thanked me deeply for my presence. A presence that meant so much that it led to the eventual baptism of this little girl's father. It was life-changing that I was just . . . there.

This experience was a total paradigm shift for me. My presence was just as important and perhaps more important than what I could say or the scriptures I could read. God summed it all up for me in a phrase that I like to use, "The ministry of the Word without the ministry of presence is not the ministry of the Word at all."

All through my ministry, I had considered myself an excellent explainer of true things. I am passionate, thoughtful, and fairly easy to understand. My churches have shown the fruit of these gifts as my districts are always at the top of my conference numbers for growth. Nevertheless, because of experiences like this one and others, I realized that I had exchanged the holy calling to be an evangelist and pastor for the attitude of a salesman. I had gotten really good at selling people a product. So I became convicted that if my heart and worldview did not change, my ministry would be full of sound and fury but would not accomplish anything.

Why did my Adventism seem so disconnected from real people in real-life situations? None of what I had been teaching was necessarily wrong, but God began to make me see that my understanding of the three angels' messages was too general. I had never really grasped the fact that although I knew how they related to end-time events in the context of the world, I did not know how they related to the context of individual hearts, real lives, actual struggles, and personal troubles. My idea of the gospel had been, more or less, summed up in the context of how a true understanding of the world's events and a person's convictions and behavior affect their eternal life. But eternal life is *then*. What about now? What about that couple that had a cocaine addiction? What about this family that lost a beloved daughter? What about my city that was in tremendous pain because a beloved middle-school staff member had been shot and killed by a Minneapolis police officer?

When Philando Castile was killed in 2016, my heart was deeply moved for his family and my city. I was also very scared about what I knew I needed to do. Twenty-four-hour protests had been going on since the shooting had hit social media. When there was so much pain happening in the city that I had called home, how could I possibly sit in my church on Sabbath and act as if everything is OK? I knew where Jesus would be on a day like that. However, I was afraid to act because in our country and in our church, people think that if you stand for one thing, you are automatically against something else. If I say black lives matter, some people take it to mean that I think blue lives or white lives do not. I felt deeply that as a pastor, I would lose the right to say that *any* lives matter if I did not try to minister to my city while it was in such pain. So we took a group of volunteers down to the protest.

I was glad for my training in crisis response because I taught my group how to handle the various potential emotions people might show us. We were not there for a political agenda; we were there for people. Just like Jesus would have been. At the end of the day, we prayed with more than twenty police officers, the mayor, and the chief of police. I was handed a megaphone and was asked to pray for the entire group of about two hundred protesters. I hugged Castile's mother, cried with his friends, and listened to people thank me that a preacher cared enough to be there.

That afternoon, I went home and collapsed in my wife's arms. The toll of the day was heavy, but I fell into her because I felt weak. I had never experienced the power of the Holy Spirit poured out like that in my entire life. Because I was present, I was able to give evidence of the truth of the gospel, and it became more real to me than ever. This event changed my preaching. I became convinced that if our message is an end-time message, then it means that it is personal for the people who are living with end-time issues. *I had to be present in the issues to realize this.*

The three angels' messages are about police shootings and racism, refugees and war. They are about comfort in disease, heartache, death, and dying, and not just in a general, doctrinal way. This message is personal and real, but it took me being present in the lives of people and in my city to realize it. When I was in the trouble, I could clearly see that only Jesus can heal hearts. When I was in the trouble, I could no longer sit from afar and judge others. When their tears were on the shoulder of my shirt, all I wanted to do was bring healing. God did not call me to run and hide from the last days; He called me to stand courageous and faithful in the midst of them. Who better to bring hope in the crisis than the people who know about the Blessed Hope?

"For God has not given us a spirit of fear, but of power and of love and of a sound mind" (2 Timothy 1:7, NKJV).

To be transparent, I had been hiding behind the façade of a message that could be taught in a neat little package over a few weeks. As long as I was affirming those teachings in my ministry, I felt that I was faithful to the call. However, it was a total denial of my duty and a retreat from the ministry of presence. I was reducing the power of God, limiting it to only exposing error, and it kept my faith all tied in a neat little bow. It was not until I was ministering in the world with my hands and feet that I began to realize the faith that I had kept fenced in limited my territory to a size that was way too small to help real people in relevant ways. It just was not practical; it reached the head, but it did not transform the entire soul.

To this day, God continues to teach me how to share this beloved message in a way that will allow for practical spiritual growth in people who are seeking Jesus. Through all of this, I have learned at least six lessons.

1. Jesus is the Truth

I have said a million times that Jesus is the center of all our teachings, but in most of my messages, that amounts to just talking about Jesus here and there. Romans 3:23–26 says that the reason God sent Jesus was to prove to us that He is righteous. "God put forward [Jesus] as a propitiation [for our sins] by his blood, to be received by faith. *This was to show God's righteousness*" (verse 25, ESV; emphasis added). He uses that phrase three times in the passage; "this was to show God's righteousness."

Paul is telling us that the solution for all the problems that make people think that God is unrighteous is not merely correct teaching, or doctrine, or ideology; it is Jesus Himself. The issues that make people believe that God is unrighteous are the exact issues that turn the world upside down at the end of time. The truth is that God does not ask us to believe in fairy tales or myths or anything else just because He said it. He asks us to believe in a Person. Today, I am called to be the evidence that Jesus is real.

This solution means that every doctrine of Scripture is not only about God. They are pieces of the person of Jesus Christ Himself. He is the Word made flesh. He is present in all truth, and He is present truth. It is not enough to tell people what is true. We need to show them how that truth is a part of their Savior. Therefore, the solution to our crumbling world is not limited to correct teaching; it is the power of God through His very presence. I have to constantly bring the person of Jesus Christ into my sermons, not merely truths that relate to Him. Jesus is not just one of the things I believe. Jesus is the embodiment of everything I believe. Jesus is not just one of the teachings among the prophecies. "The testimony of Jesus is the spirit of prophecy" (Revelation 19:10).

Ellen White says it this way:

The only way in which men will be able to stand firm in the conflict is to be rooted and grounded in Christ. They must receive the truth as it is in Jesus. And it is only as the truth is presented thus that it can meet the wants of the soul. The preaching of Christ crucified, Christ our righteousness, is what satisfies the soul's hunger. When we secure the interest of the people in this great central truth, faith and hope and courage come to the heart.[1]

2. Daniel and Revelation are *not the only theme* by which the truth may be presented

In the past, my first few nights during an evangelistic series were usually on prophecy, but the meetings very quickly took a turn for testing truths. Cannot testing truths show up in many areas of life and Scripture? For example, when we take a deeper look at what we believe about Christ's ministry in heaven, we see that the judgment is the solution for racism, injustice, and hate. After all, Jesus is in heaven to unite our hearts with the heavenly sanctuary. He is there not to condemn but to free us, to rid us of the sinfulness that divides us. Jesus' return is the final act where, finally, it is all made right. Every act of protest, even misguided, is a cry for the justice and judgment of God. While 1844 is important, what Jesus is accomplishing during the judgment in this time of crisis is more important than the date.

One of my most successful evangelistic series came after I attended the Castile protests. The entire theme was on racism, injustice, and God's judgment. These issues had me digging deep about every important truth that I would normally teach in a series.

Ultimately, my goal in a meeting is to reveal God's true character. Understood properly, the character of God is the solution to real end-time issues. Why not meet these issues head-on with the message of God's character?

To many people, only teaching prophecy is beating around the bush. It paints too broad a picture. It is not personal and, at times, seems irrelevant. If

I say Jesus is the answer, that does not mean that Jesus is a part of the answer. It means He is the whole answer. If I present a truth of Scripture as the answer to an issue, I had better be able to show how that answer is a part of Jesus Himself. To better understand the three angels' messages in these last days, the answer is not to withdraw from the issues; it is to get my hands dirty in them. Jesus shows up every time, and my preaching is transformed.

3. My presence in people's lives is the key to preaching

I am constantly talking with my members and their small groups to find out what they are talking about, what their neighbors are asking them, and what topics come up at work, and what else is relevant to them. Great sermon topics come from listening to how other people process current events and issues. Sitting with them in trials and struggles forces me to think about how I think and process my faith. The more I am present in the lives of other people, the bigger the gospel becomes to me, and the more it applies to end-time issues. For too long, as an Adventist, I had not mingled with people; I had tried to put on great programs that would make people want to mingle with me. This approach could not produce transformative end-time preaching.

4. I need to leave room for a little doubt and wonder

People do not have to agree with every point of every sermon. Expecting this makes me seem like a know-it-all. I must acknowledge how complicated life can be. Affirming how challenging personal struggles can be makes my messages more genuine.

True faith leaves room for doubt. God praised Job at the end of his story, even though Job got angry and questioned God. He also condemned Job's friends, who tried to come up with explanations that gave a false picture of God's character.

After the Resurrection, Thomas's issue was not doubt; it was certainty. He would not believe unless he was made certain by putting his hands on the risen Jesus.

God is much bigger and glorious than my mind can ever fathom. Sometimes, saying "I don't know" can save my soul and others' too. As a preacher, I need to be OK with that. Preaching about things that perplex me and being willing to be vulnerable with my pain and battles creates an instant bond with people who want a preacher with whom they can relate. Acknowledging how complicated a person's situation is actually opens the heart. Having an answer for everything or an argument for everything belittles people. Having an answer for everything makes me seem distant. Having doubt makes me seem present.

5. I need to preach about truth

For many years, I believed that preaching truth came from exposing error. I can remember preaching for forty-five minutes to prove other denominations wrong and for ten minutes about Jesus before I was to make an appeal. I am called as a preacher of the gospel to lift up Jesus. I have discovered that, when Christ is lifted up, error gets exposed as a by-product. Present truth is bringing God's true character into the present.

God's character is not lifted up by exposing error; it is lifted up by telling people what is true. There are occasions to address questions and errors, but I have found that these occur much less frequently than I have believed in the past. I used to get people who would argue with me after sermons. I had one guy stand up during a meeting and try to argue with me. Looking back, I can see it was because I had offended him by directly arguing against what He believed. Now simply sharing with people what is true and beautiful has made far fewer enemies and increased positive results and more decisions. People are hungry for what is true.

6. Context is everything

One of the biggest mistakes I have made in my ministry is expecting the same things to work in the same ways in every place. This expectation is just not reality. After pastoring in three different parts of the United States and having ministered on several mission trips, I have been astounded at how different we humans can be. There are thousands of subcultures in North America alone. It is unreasonable to expect to step into an area and understand how to communicate without much research. Therefore, being present at community events, getting to know neighbors, attending city government meetings, partnering with established service organizations, playing sports in local recreation leagues, and sitting aside to listen to conversations at cafés are vitally important to my ministry. In recent years, I have invested in demographic research to get to know important details about my area. In the past, I had not realized how different my worldview could be from the person sitting across from me. We may both be speaking English, but it is possible not to be communicating at all because of the dichotomy in the way we see the world.

Conclusion

Ministry has taught me that the reason God called me is not that I am holy or intelligent but that He perhaps has more work to do on me than He does other people. He calls me into my city and into the lives of people because He knows that this is exactly what has to be done to make Himself more real to me. The more real Jesus is to me, the more effective I can be in helping people live through this great controversy. Truth, for me, is no longer just things that are true. Truth, for me, is a Person.

---

1. "Sabbath, January 28: Sabbath Services," *General Conference Daily Bulletin* 5, no. 1 (January 27, 28, 1893): 14.

Dustin Hall is the lead pastor at the Port Charlotte Seventh-day Adventist Church in Florida. He has a unique ability to show how Seventh-day Adventist beliefs are best understood by and communicated to people outside the church. He has pastored churches in rural, urban, and suburban contexts where deep community involvement has been central to growth.

Born Again Blindness: Why People Don't See the Gospel as Good News, Part 1
Video Presentation (RT: 24:45)
Dustin Hall

Born Again Blindness: Why People Don't See the Gospel as Good News, Part 2
Video Presentation (RT: 10:21)
Dustin Hall

CHAPTER 9

Follow Up Your Interests Through Baptism and Discipleship

John T. Boston II

Misty was eleven years old and the daughter of a Baptist minister. Her mother's current husband was also a former lay pastor in the Baptist faith tradition. She and her family were no longer active in any faith. When she responded to the appeal to be baptized as a student at an Adventist academy week of worship, we were happy for her and immediately scheduled a visit with her parents. At that visit, Misty let us know that she wanted to be a Seventh-day Adventist. She had already talked about this with her parents, and they were fully prepared to support her decision.

In preparation for her baptism, the school chaplain and I worked with Misty to draft a short message and an appeal for others to respond to God's call on their lives. I learned many years ago that it is not a sermon if there is not an appeal. Without an appeal, it is just a lecture. The day came. She spoke, made the appeal, and got baptized. At her appeal, others responded, and in the following months, they were also baptized, and she helped lead their baptismal studies!

Several weeks later, Misty asked us to plan to stop by her house and speak with her mother. Unbeknownst to us, Misty had been having conversations with her mother and encouraging her faith journey. This lovely young lady decided that it was time that her mother decided to surrender all to God again, for good this time. We arrived at the house and prayed before we went in. The family was as pleasant as always. The chaplain I was working with had a seat, and after a cordial conversation, he made a pointed statement to the mother: "Misty tells us that she believes you are ready to make a decision to follow in her footsteps and be baptized. I agree with her. You're ready, and I'd like to schedule your baptism date now."

This was a no-holds-barred situation. The silence was deafening, and then came the response. "Yes. Yes, I am." Out of sheer curiosity, I asked how her husband would feel about this. Her response was priceless: "I have to stand before God on my own. My daughter was willing to take her stand, and now I am willing to take mine and be a part of the Adventist Church." I was completely floored and could not do anything but jump from my seat and wrap my arms around her.

What if we had not made the appeal for baptism at the school? What if there was no appeal from Misty at the church? What if there was no appeal at home? There are three major takeaways from this experience that I want to share with you:

1. Make appeals for baptism a part of the local ministry culture.
2. Organize your retention plan as a part of the reaping process. This makes evangelism transformational instead of transactional.
3. Identify the connection points in your church where people will plug in and grow.

I believe if your ministry practices these elements, you will have more success in evangelism than any budget could pay for.

A culture of appeals

When regular appeals are made, it becomes a part of the local ministry expression. We must do everything we can to nurture an environment conducive to response, but the response is always by the power of the Holy Spirit. Our responsibility is not for conviction but for proclamation. We must not try to carry the burden of success based on the number of people that respond. We must consider ourselves successful by the clarity, consistency, and boldness of our appeals. Misty and the chaplain had become accustomed to an appeal being made, so their approach to discipling those around them included an appeal.

If your ministry has been disingenuous and you were only trying to get a decision for numbers' sake, then a no response is a failure. However, if you are genuinely making an appeal to connect a wandering heart to the loving Savior, then a no response won't stop the ministry. I've been told no more times than I can count, but I didn't stop loving and caring and visiting. That's because the appeal is not a measure of your persuasive prowess. The appeal is how you express your confidence in what you have just shared about the power of the gospel.

In 2013, I led one of the largest public evangelistic meetings in North America. Between two sites, we hosted well over five thousand people in central Georgia. I invited an NFL player and a television personality to share their testimonies. I preached the Second Coming message and made an appeal at the end. It was terrible. Hardly anyone responded, and I was utterly embarrassed after all the effort that went into pulling off that event.

Each night I kept preaching and making appeals, and in the end, seventy-six people were baptized that summer because of those events. One of my church elders came to me at the end of it all and said something I will never forget: "Pastor, I know you thought a ton of people were going to come up for baptism on opening night. You were discouraged, but look at what God did! He blessed us because you faithfully kept making the appeals. God doesn't bless us because of our plans; He blesses us because of our faithfulness." Be faithful in making appeals. You won't regret it.

I heard a story maybe twenty years ago:

A great evangelist was approached by a young minister with a query. He asked the evangelist why so many people responded to his appeals. The seasoned veteran asked him, "Do you expect people to come every time you make an appeal?"

The young preacher answered, "No, not every time."

The evangelist replied, "That's your problem. There are always people in need of the Savior. He's always calling for them to come home, and, in the appeal, you make sure they know it."

In prayer meetings, Sabbath School, Pathfinder gatherings, funerals, home visits, Bible studies, and anywhere else you can, always make an appeal. The Word of God is powerful, and when it is presented, it warrants a response. Even when I falter in my sermon preparation, I make an appeal. You may never have that chance again to make the call, and those in the audience may not have another chance to hear it. If you look closely at the ministry of Jesus, you will see many appeals. I love the simplicity of the first three words in Matthew 11:28, "Come unto me." If your sermon or study doesn't have this in it, you may be missing the mark.

Next, we will consider the significance of organizing the retention plan as a part of the evangelistic process.

Appeals and retention

Unfortunately, many churches organize their evangelism practices as events. They engage and disengage, like the transmission of a car. Evangelism must be seen as the engine and not the transmission. The church is either "on" in the soul-winning process or "off" like the motor of a vehicle. Therefore, retention must be planned along with the different phases of evangelism. We don't win in baptisms; we win in follow-up. If the efforts following a series or ministry happening are not given as much attention as the event itself, you are bound to lose the majority of those who decide to be baptized. In some instances, it would be better not to host an evangelistic event than to do so without a plan for retention. Failure to do so is spiritual malpractice.

Connection points

"Baptism is not the end of evangelism. Once persons have found the knowledge of this wonderful Adventist message, the next step is to bring them into full fellowship with the church and invite them on a journey toward discipleship through active evangelism. Transformational evangelism never ends! It is a cycle that continues forever."[1] There are probably countless ways to do this. I would like to share my practice of creating connection points to remedy the attrition of new converts. I believe that following this approach has the potential to close the proverbial back door of the church, where so many have departed from their newfound faith.

Connection points are circumstances in which people plug in and experience the full fellowship of the local church. Connection points must include all three of the following to qualify as a proper place to plug in and grow:

1. They must be *collaborative* in nature.
2. They must *nurture* spiritual growth.
3. They must be *Great Commission* oriented.

Connection points are collaborative in nature. A collaborative ministry must include multiple ministry leaders and team members. These ministries can be internal and/or external. Youth ministry is a great example. In a more traditional context, the leaders of the Pathfinder group, youth Sabbath School, and family ministry should together be organizing the ministry efforts for the young people. Working together fosters a team atmosphere focused on a specific demographic. Their efforts should include all young people in the community, not just those who are members of the church. Are not the children in the community just as important as those attending church? Events, worship experiences, and Bible studies should be coordinated together. This approach gives a united front for the work of discipling young people. It also provides a higher level of consistency across the board with a ministry as significant as youth ministry.

It is important to ensure that the days of "territorial ministry" are at an immediate and abrupt end. If ministry leaders in your church will not work well with others for the greater good, talk seriously with them and help them find an area of service that requires limited to no interaction with others. In all truthfulness, if ministry leaders can only do it their way, the problem is deeper than we can cover in this short chapter. All leaders and team members in the local church must exhibit an amenable spirit when it comes to working together. Nothing kills a good thing like a toxic team member. It's not easy, but find ways to deal with this so that healthy collaboration can take place. The more an idea can survive the filters of others, the better it becomes.

Connection points nurture spiritual growth. The collaboration element does not address the spiritual nurture component. Both must be present to make a connection point. For example, I love block parties. Block parties are collaborative, and they help reach our community. Their nature makes block parties Great Commission oriented. Unfortunately, the prayers at the beginning and over the food don't make block parties spiritual. Block parties are an absolutely wonderful way to connect, but they are not connection points in the sense we are exploring because they do not directly provide spiritual nurture. Remember, a connection point must provide all three elements.

So what does spiritual nurture look like? Glad you asked.

Spiritual nurture directly addresses the human condition of separation from God. I will admit that I have been to Bible studies that were more about us being right than about Jesus, so nurture is not just the study of scriptures. Spiritual nurture is concerned about how well someone is connected to Christ and His body, growth in His Word, and compassion for self and others. In the book *Finding Them, Keeping Them*, Gary McIntosh and Glen Martin reference Lyle E. Schaller's research on inclusion. "Fundamentally, there are two separate levels of inclusion. One is superficial and the other relational. Involvement and accountability are the signatures of relational inclusion for healthy assimilation in the local church. These must be constantly nurtured."[2] This is where spiritual nurture is such an essential component of connection. The growth that occurs through involvement is anchored by sharing the principles of God's Word.

This spiritual nurture component can be exercised in a plethora of ways, but some of the most common spiritual nurture activities are Christ-centered, practical themes for everyday living. My favorites include marriage enrichment, Bible study, spiritual dialogue, intergenerational gatherings where life and the love of Christ are the focus, and team-building activities that draw heavily on biblical principles for learning. This list is not for limiting spiritual nurture but, rather, provides some ideas for where you might begin. The Sabbath worship experience, among other things, is one of the spiritual nurture cornerstones, but please do not limit yourself to this once-per-week event.

Connection points are Great Commission oriented. Finally, the connection points must be Great Commission oriented. This is a big component of how you identify and practice your approach to discipleship and baptism. Fundamentally, we must push out into the community of which we are a part. Our ministries should and must reflect the communities we serve. If we look around on a Sabbath and see only our members, it should incite within us a desire to reevaluate our efforts. If we are the only ones in the pews, we are a club and not a church.

Every facet of ministry planning should begin with the question, "How will this reach the community around our center of faith?" The answer may mean you have to shut down some efforts to build up others—especially those that work better in this context. Our church is notorious for planning conferences and special days. Put that energy into organizing plans that are designed for both members and the community (future members). This is how interests plug in and grow. They recognize in their spiritual journey that joining the church does not separate them from the community. Joining the church elevates their sense of community to a level of spiritual responsibility.

"Community visitation is not to be confused with community visibility. Community visitation concentrates on the direct interaction and direct involvement with community residents."[3] Sabbath School, Pathfinders, Sabbath morning worship, prayer meeting, and Adventist Youth Society should be filled with people who are not yet members. If this isn't happening, go back to God and try again. Would it be dynamic if your church's family ministry department became the positive leader for families in your city? What if your Pathfinder ministry was the city's go-to mentoring solution for young people? How about collaborating with Whole Foods to host a lifestyle class? This can happen only if you are going out and visiting with the people. Once they join, don't stop. Keep visiting and nurturing the bond because you don't just care about their decision; you care about their journey.

When I work with local churches to identify their connection points, I always make home visits one of those. For far too long, we have measured someone's connection by how often they come to us. A home visit flips that and helps us measure their connection by how often we go to them. As a matter of good practice, your connection points should have as strong a representation of the members going to a new believer as they have of the new believer coming to the events of the church.

Conclusion

Above are some of the ways you can push out to be a part of the community to which you are called to minister. Salt cannot impact the flavor of food unless it is mixed in. Light does not affect darkness unless it shines among the shadows. "Christ's method alone will give true success in reaching the people. The Saviour mingled with men as one who desired their good. He showed His sympathy for them, ministered to their needs, and won their confidence. Then He bade them, 'Follow Me.' "[4]

Again, here are the three elements for building a connection point:

1. They must be *collaborative* in nature.
2. They must *nurture* spiritual growth.
3. They must be *Great Commission* oriented.

List the ministries you have that possess all three of these elements. Once you have that list, place the name of each person that plugs into them in a column under the connection point. If you keep those persons plugged in to at least three places over the course of three months, I guarantee the number of connections will grow.

For following up our interests for baptism, we have discussed three components:

1. Make appeals for baptism a part of the local ministry culture.
2. Organize your retention plan as a part of the reaping process. Planning this way makes evangelism transformational instead of transactional.
3. Identify the connection points in your church where people will plug in and grow.

If you look closely at this, you will see that it requires a lot of work. You are right! It takes a labor of love to engage in this type of transformational evangelism. It does not turn on in the summer and off the rest of the year. It keeps going and going, just like the love of God. If it were easy, everyone would do it. If you tune in your ear, you will find that our conversations increase around revitalization as our engagement around evangelism decreases. We can turn this ship around and have the dynamic impact of the early church if we take on the challenge of the great work with the commitment to be faithful.

As you plan for the future, I would like to admonish you to put a great deal of energy into how you follow up. This is where true success lies. Make the appeals, precisely plan your retention, and organize your connection points. In turn, you and your members will see an increase in the number of decisions and disciples that follow. "Press toward the mark for the prize of the high calling of God in Christ Jesus" (Philippians 3:14, KJV).

Useful Resources

Books

Brantley, Paul, Dan Jackson, and Mike Cauley. *Becoming a Mission-Driven Church: A Five-Step Strategy for Moving Your Church From Ordinary to Exceptional.* Nampa ID: Pacific Press®, 2015.

Byrd, Carlton P. *Contemporary Evangelism for the 21st Century.* Nampa, ID: Pacific Press®, 2018.

McIntosh, Gary, and Glen Martin. *Finding Them, Keeping Them.* Nashville, TN: B&H Books, 1991.

---

1. Paul Brantley, Dan Jackson, and Mike Cauley, *Becoming a Mission Driven Church* (Nampa, ID: Pacific Press®, 2015), 199.

2. Gary McIntosh and Glen Martin, *Finding Them, Keeping Them* (Nashville, TN: B&H Books, 1991), 76.

3. Carlton P. Byrd, *Contemporary Evangelism for the 21st Century* (Nampa, ID: Pacific Press®, 2018), 93.

4. Ellen G. White, *The Ministry of Healing* (Mountain View, CA: Pacific Press®, 1942), 143.

John T. Boston II is an associate director for the North American Division Evangelism Institute at Andrews University. He is responsible for field schools and public evangelism education at the Seventh-day Adventist Theological Seminary and across the North American Division. He has also served as school evangelist for the North New South Wales Conference in Australia. He holds a bachelor of arts in ministerial theology from Oakwood University and a master of arts in peace and social justice with an emphasis in interfaith action from Claremont Lincoln University. He is currently enrolled in the Doctor of Missiology program at Andrews University.

Connection Points
Video Presentation (RT: 19:58)
John T. Boston II

ACTION 4—EQUIP

Multiply through

mentoring members

who make disciples.

Shaken Baby Syndrome

Jose Cortes Jr.

*"Go therefore and make disciples of all the nations, baptizing them in
the name of the Father and of the Son and of the Holy Spirit, teaching
them to observe all things that I have commanded you; and lo,
I am with you always, even to the end of the age." Amen.*
—Matthew 28:19, 20, NKJV

When babies are born, they do not know everything; neither can they do everything! They need help. The same happens with spiritual babies after their new birth and baptism.

I learned this the hard way one night a few days after my son Jose Cortes III was born. As I heard him crying through the little TV monitor on the side table of our bedroom, I woke up my wife and said, "Baby, Jose III is crying; he is probably hungry."

My wife, Joanne, replied in her sleep, "He is not hungry; I just fed him; it's your turn to check on him."

So there I went, ready to comfort my little boy in the middle of the night.

As I got to his room, I tried to smile at him and talk to him; you know, the way people talk to babies, "What's happening to my little Bubbah baby? Papa loves yoouuuu!"

You know how people get with babies. I did all of that, and the more I talked to him, the more he cried! He was not having any of my baby talk. Finally, I noticed he was wet. I softly picked him up and placed him on the brand-new changing table. After I undid and removed his diaper, I positioned myself really close to him, put my finger on his chest, and began to baby talk again. Now he smiled at me. Just as I felt my five-day-old baby and I were having the best bonding time ever, a warm fluid shot with tremendous accuracy, freezing my smile as it hit my face and mouth. I could not believe it! I do not remember ever having had that experience before in my life. I was unhappy for a moment, left the baby on the changing table (something my wife scolded me for later on), and ran for the bathroom to wash my mouth and face. As I came back, I saw my baby totally helpless and still dirty on top of that changing table. I could have yelled at him; I could have said harsh words; I could have shaken him, as some parents do, causing irreparable "shaken baby syndrome." However, I realized he had just been born, and my love and my help were what he needed.

When babies are born, they can make a mess and lots of noise, but they cannot talk, eat on their own, clean themselves, or walk, among many other things. This helplessness is why babies need the utmost care, love, and instruction. They need equipping and the opportunity to start developing their abilities in order to grows, matures, and, one day, reproduce. The same applies to spiritual babies. Baptism represents the birth, and the discipleship journey is the growth process, leading the new believer to become stronger in the faith and to reproduce.

Evangelism Action 4—Equip
Multiply through mentoring members who make disciples.

From 2015 to 2020, we surveyed and talked with thousands of pastors, members, and church leaders. Our study resulted in six actions that could revolutionize mission and evangelism across North America. Eighty-eight percent ranked "equip" at 7 or higher on a 1–10 scale.

There is a danger in believing that baptism is the graduation, or a final step, rather than a new beginning. We think that when people get baptized, our work is done, and we forget all about them. Perhaps this is one reason why some people we baptize end up leaving the church. According to the latest statistics from the church Secretariat, we lose thirty-nine of every one hundred we baptize. This statistic demonstrates the importance of each church developing an intentional discipleship path for the newly baptized as well as for existing members.

Equipping our members to partner with and count on the presence of the Holy Spirit as we grow in Christ and teaching them that our biblical beliefs are gifts from God, rather than a checklist for baptism, are vital in the discipleship journey. Small groups and life groups provide healthy and safe settings for not only reaching new converts but also helping both new and veteran believers experience life, prayer, praise, and Bible study. Together, they may learn the importance of a witnessing lifestyle in the workplace and neighborhood.

Through the years, there have been some who thought that discipleship is the mere knowledge of our twenty-eight fundamental beliefs. While I believe this is key and that we have the most complete and comprehensive package of beliefs of any church, it must be clear that knowledge alone does not make someone a disciple. A disciple of Jesus constantly learns His teachings, loves and serves people, leads sinners to salvation by grace, and reproduces by mentoring and empowering new believers to become disciples.

Understanding that new converts are not finished products—but babies in the faith, who need love, care, and equipping—could help the church to sharply increase their survival rate. Perhaps this would keep them from dying of spiritual "shaken baby syndrome" at the hands of church members who still have not understood the value of a soul. An intentional discipleship path could, perhaps, make the greatest difference between those who stay and those who leave the church after baptism. Besides, it could also help transform the lives of longtime church members who are simply warming pews or those who argue their theological pet peeves without having contributed to leading a single person to Christ in decades.

Next time you see someone being baptized into your church family, keep in mind that babies do not know everything and cannot do a whole lot on their own. That is why God created parents, older brothers and sisters, and a church family. Please do not shake him, do not yell at her, even if they get you dirty. Do not forget: your church family does not exist to neglect spiritual newborns but to love them, teach them, equip them, and help them become disciples who will make more disciples.

Jose Cortes III, the five-day-old baby that shot warm fluids into my mouth as I was trying to clean him up on that night that shall forever live in infamy, has grown to be a teenager. Now he can talk, eat on his own, take his showers, cut the grass, care for a dog, play several instruments and sports, and even help us clean the house every Friday. And he is not done growing yet. We cannot wait to see what else God is going to do with him.

Please discuss this evangelism action with your church and how to make it a reality in your setting. What can your church do to set up an intentional discipleship path for the benefit of its new converts and longtime members? How can your church equip members who make disciples?

CHAPTER 10

Make Disciples Who Make Disciples

Abdiel Del Toro

I grew up in a church where they always talked about "adding" more people, but they never talked about "multiplying." That church offered many activities and programs—from events for children and young people to concerts and "weeks of evangelism." I am grateful to God for the experiences that I had in my church.

For many, there was nothing wrong with this church model. On the contrary, it was normal and acceptable. In retrospect, I realize that the leaders were always the same, and the church had very little variation in the number of attendees. People were baptized, but there was no plan for the new converts. After analyzing this, I came to believe that it was not that we had bad intentions; it was that we were not intentional enough.

Today I am convinced that the problem of that particular church, and many others, is this: a bad definition of the Great Commission keeps us very active as a church, but we fail to fulfill the purpose for which we exist. Many believers today are very busy in their congregations. They have many responsibilities. There are many events. Church calendars lack the space to add more activities. Nevertheless, all that movement does not necessarily make us what God wants us to be.

God's dream for us is to be disciples who make disciples
While Jesus performed His public ministry here on earth, His call to people was always to follow Him. He did so with Matthew, Philip, Peter, John, and others. To those who chose and accepted His call, Christ dedicated His three and a half years of ministry. Jesus walked on earth, preaching the good news of the kingdom, performing miracles, and carrying out His Messianic work. In

addition to that, the Savior dedicated all His time to His disciples. He taught them privately, prayed with them, ate with them, modeled the ministry, revealed the gospel, corrected them, empowered them, and sent them out on a mission. The Lord Jesus invested in their lives so that when His time on earth ended, they would continue with the mission He had begun.

Christ was intentional about multiplying in the life of His disciples
After those three and a half years, Jesus died and rose again. The time of His ministry on earth was over, but His mission was just beginning. At that moment, Christ gave a direct command to His disciples. Matthew 28:18–20 records the greatest mission statement that the Master of Galilee pronounced while on this earth.

The Great Commission was not a suggestion. And it was not just for those disciples. It was the revelation of God's great plan for His church: "Make disciples!" The risen Savior told His disciples to go, to baptize, and to teach, but the result of all that was to make disciples. "Go" was important, as were "baptizing" and "teaching," but the essential plan was for His disciples to go and make more disciples, who, in turn, would do so as witnesses of God to the end of the world.

Jesus wanted—and He still wants—His disciples to do the same thing He did with them: invest in the lives of others and make them disciples who will go around the world, making more disciples for the kingdom. They took the command to heart, and that is exactly what they did. The Word of God says in Acts 6:7, "So the word of God spread. The number of disciples in Jerusalem increased rapidly, and a large number of priests became obedient to the faith" (NIV).

The disciples dedicated their lives to fulfilling the Lord's command to make disciples. Those, in turn, did their part and continued to make more disciples. This divine plan has not changed. God's dream for His children remains the same. God wants each of us to follow Him, as His disciples did, while dedicating our lives to multiplying—working in others' lives so that they, too, can grow in the experience of discipleship. Jesus' great plan is that this process continues until His second coming.

A great example to follow—the story of a modern disciple
Rogelio Llaurador is an example of a disciple who has understood the definition of the Great Commission well. His story is a very inspiring. Rogelio was not born in a religious home, and the gospel was not part of his early formation. At the age of twenty, he began a new stage in his life. He married and

moved away from that nonreligious environment. Years later, in 1961, Rogelio moved with his family to Queens, New York. On several occasions, he visited the Adventist church, but no one ever took the initiative to ask him if he knew Jesus, or if he would like to. Everyone assumed that this was a fact. After he had visited the church many times, finally, a disciple, convinced of the Great Commission, asked Rogelio if he knew Jesus or would like to get to know Him. That same day, not during the sermon, nor during Sabbath School, but in a conversation in a hallway, Rogelio decided to learn more about Jesus.

Each Tuesday became a special day in which that "committed disciple" visited Rogelio and spent time with him. They shared and learned together about the Savior. As time went by, Rogelio began to know and trust God as never before. His decision to be baptized was slow in coming, but little by little, he was spiritually growing. During the entire process, the "committed disciple" never abandoned him.

Years went by, and one day Rogelio felt that God had other plans for him and was leading him to move to another city. He moved to Orlando, Florida. Providentially, while in Orlando, God placed a young man named Frank González (who later became the speaker of the Voice of Prophecy ministry in Spanish, Voz de la Esperanza) in Rogelio's path. González befriended him and invited him to visit his church. When Rogelio arrived at the church, he was surprised at how well he was received, accepted, and loved from day one.

In November 1976, that love and intentional friendship led Rogelio to give his life to God and become a disciple of Jesus through baptism. From that moment on, he desired to bring others to experience the love of God. Rogelio went from being a colporteur to being one of the pioneers of the Westchester Adventist Church in the city of Miami. He dedicated his life to following Christ as a disciple, making disciples.

Rogelio, a disciple who multiplies
I met Rogelio some time ago through his participation in a project implemented by the Southern Union and the Florida Conference. The project sought to equip church elders to take a more significant role in the mission of the church and, at the same time, serve as model disciples for the local congregations. This annual project authorizes church elders, on a scheduled Sabbath date, to baptize those with whom they have been investing time. This project is a blessing in our territory. In the first year it was carried out (2017), the Florida Conference Hispanic churches' elders baptized more than 150 people. Rogelio is one of the elders who, every year since then, has baptized precious souls. In

the last two years alone, Rogelio baptized more than 20 people! He has the vision of a disciple who seeks to multiply. His example in the church has been impressive. Rogelio's passion and commitment to the Great Commission are evident and worthy of imitation.

While talking with him one day, I asked how he made the Great Commission his way of life and how he brought so many people to Christ. His answer greatly impacted my heart. Rogelio said, "First, I pray to God, every day, to put someone in my path whom I can talk to about Him. However, God has never given me just one. There are always more. I ask God to give me grace toward people. Second, I never miss an opportunity to share Jesus with the people I meet. I always make it a point to serve them." He continued, "I never take for granted that people know Jesus. I ask them if they know Him. I talk to God about everyone I meet along the way. The last baptism in the Westchester Spanish Church was for a man I met while at the clinic. I befriended him, and we ended up talking about God. From that friendship, we began to study the Bible. After several months, that friend came to church and then decided to be baptized!

"The third thing I do is interact with people, which I love doing, even when they have not decided for Jesus yet. (Later, after they are baptized, I interact with them even more.) I exchange text messages every day with my friends who are not from church because I want them to know that they are valuable to God. I send them Bible promises. Again, once they are baptized, I continue the friendship and spend time with them frequently, studying the Bible, helping them to know Jesus at a deeper level, praying together, and even teaching them how the Adventist Church works. I want them to know how the church manages tithe and how they can get involved in church leadership. I encourage them to participate in church decision-making, in administrative meetings, and to get involved in sharing their faith and their Savior with others."

While contemplating Rogelio's words, I once more confirmed in my heart that being a disciple who multiplies is the only way to live the gospel, to live Christianity, and to live Adventism. Hearing the passion with which this man spoke to me and his conversion story made me think, *That should be the experience of each believer.* I am convinced that God calls us to *live* the Great Commission and not to make it an occasional activity. God wants us to be disciples who multiply!

Practical lessons
Drawing from Rogelio's experiences of how to live under the banner of the Great Commission, I would like to expand on three lessons that seem vital

to me. I am sure these lessons will also apply to those of you who desire to be disciples who multiply.

1. Disciples who make disciples begin with God. It caught my attention when I heard Rogelio say that every day he asks God to put someone in his path so he can talk with them about the gospel. It seems that we often miss the basics when we talk about fulfilling the Great Commission. *It starts with God!* What if, before we discuss religious strategies, we start spending time alone with God? We should seek His presence and ask Him to show us whom He has been working with, and where, so we can be at the right place and time to support His work. God is diligently at work on His mission of saving the world. He is at work in every human heart even before we reach a soul.

Multiplying disciples listen to God's voice and are guided by His plan. The book of Acts records two experiences of Paul that help us to understand this concept. The passages read as follows: "During the night Paul had a vision of a man of Macedonia standing and begging him, 'Come over to Macedonia and help us.' After Paul had seen the vision, we got ready at once to leave for Macedonia, concluding that God had called us to preach the gospel to them" (Acts 16:9, 10, NIV).

"One night, the Lord spoke to Paul in a vision: 'Do not be afraid; keep on speaking, do not be silent. For I am with you, and no one is going to attack and harm you, because I have many people in this city.' So Paul stayed in Corinth for a year and a half, teaching them the word of God" (Acts 18:9–11, NIV).

Here, we see that Paul moved forward on his mission because God confirmed that it was the place where the people he should invest in were. If we want to be intentional in growing as multiplying disciples, we must begin by asking God to take us to the people He has in mind for us.

2. Disciples are intentional in relating to and investing in people. If there is a key to Rogelio's success, it is that he relates to people and is intentionally determined to be a multiplying disciple. Let me expound a little more on this point. God is a real and relational Being. He wants us to know Him, and knowing Him is eternal life (John 17:3).

God desires to have a deep and personal relationship with all who approach Him. A disciple who makes disciples for Jesus grows in a personal relationship with Him and then makes Him known to others through personal testimony as we interact with them. Without good relationships, and without intentionality in relating and loving people, the Great Commission becomes mere proselytizing. The gospel is not just information; it is a life experience that develops as we relate to God and to our neighbor.

Intentional relationships with people allow us to preach with no need for a sermon and teach without Bible studies. We share our testimony and show how God will work in them as well. I am not saying here that we should not preach or teach the Word of God. What I am saying is that, through relationships with people, we can model the gospel, showing that they can live better because the gospel offers something better. Ellen White's famous quote regarding the method of Christ highlights Jesus' intentional purpose for relationships: "Christ's method alone will give true success in reaching the people. The Saviour mingled with men as one who desired their good. He showed His sympathy for them, ministered to their needs, and won their confidence. Then He bade them, 'Follow Me.' "[1]

The quote says that Christ *mingled with people, showed them sympathy, ministered to their needs*, and *earned their confidence*. How could all this be achieved without intentionally relating to people? Disciples who make disciples will be intentional about developing relationships with the people God places before them.

3. Disciples who multiply do not disconnect from their disciples. When I spoke with Rogelio, something important resonated in my heart. He firmly stated the value of maintaining a relationship with people even after they are baptized. Sometimes, we believers who have been in church for a long time have developed a mindset of *adding* to the church and not of *multiplying* the church. The problem is that we have turned the baptism into a finish point when it really is a new birth! Adding more members and reaching targets has become an end in itself. However, the goal is not to *add* members but to *multiply* disciples. Disciples only multiply if there is continued growth. Growth requires mentoring, follow-up, and relationship building not based solely on the individual's acceptance of my religion. If we focused more on walking with new believers, helping them to grow as disciples who make disciples and teaching them to multiply and live the Great Commission, our churches would be very different. Adding is not the ultimate purpose of our mission; it is only a step in the multiplication process. The ultimate goal is to have disciples intentionally making disciples, who in turn, will continue the cycle of multiplication, creating discipling communities in every city and every corner of the planet! For that to happen, we must stop practicing the religion of isolation and learn how to make the church a community again.

Multiplying is ideal

Disciples making disciples is God's plan. It is His mandate for us. The Lord wants to see His children rise and seize their identity as disciples of Christ multiplying everywhere. That identity will give new meaning to church and a vision for real growth. God does not want us to continue defining the church as a building, nor as a program, nor as a weekend activity. The desire of our Redeemer is for us to understand that church is a community of disciples living and growing in the presence of Jesus, investing their lives in the lives of others so that they, too, can live and grow in Jesus. In essence, the church is disciples who make disciples.

1. Ellen G. White, *The Ministry of Healing* (Mountain View, CA: Pacific Press®, 1942), 143.

Abdiel del Toro is the vice president for Hispanic Ministries at the Florida Conference. He has served as an Adventist pastor for the last fifteen years both in Florida and his homeland of Puerto Rico.

Multiplication
Video Presentation (RT: 15:47)
Abdiel Del Toro

Chapter 11

Engage All Members in Small Groups

Vanessa Hairston

H ave you ever been in a room full of people yet felt completely and utterly alone? It's safe to say we have all felt like this at one time or another. Perhaps it was at a new school when you were younger or a family reunion with people you did not really want to see. Or maybe, unfortunately, it was in a church. I have often heard stories of people, both Adventist and non-Adventist, who feel like, when they come to church, they do so to sit, listen, and then go home, feeling as lonely as they were when they walked in. This superficial culture easily entraps churches who rely solely on congregational worship as their connection point in the week. Sabbath consists of a fraction of our Saturday, with some exceptions for the monthly potluck, and we return home to our families, roommates, or empty living spaces. If you look at the life of Jesus, He lived a life full of enriching relationships stemming from the Trinity, where He was living in community at all times. Is it a wonder that He sought the same thing on earth?

We see Jesus engaged in small groups at varying levels. He had followers in almost every city. Seventy-two of them committed to His ministry. He chose a group of twelve by name. And lastly, He had three with whom He shared His most intimate moments (Matthew 26:37). We see Him crash at the house of Mary and Martha, where they shared food, fellowship, and several teachable moments. Jesus was benefited greatly by being in the presence of people, especially in intimate settings. The feeding-of-the-five-thousand moments were necessary, but so were intimately shared moments with people Jesus knew and who knew Him.

John recorded one of these moments. Jesus had just busted open the gates of hell with His death-defying resurrection, and Mary was outside His tomb, grieving the loss of her beloved Teacher and Friend. The angels gave her a heads-up of where Jesus was, but even upon seeing Him, she did not immediately recognize Him. Supposing He was there to brush off the dirt from the stone or freshen up the flowers, she desperately begged Him, "Sir, if you have carried him away, tell me where you have put him, and I will get him"(John 20:15, NIV). One can only imagine the tone of how Jesus said the next word, "Mary." The Bible says she immediately recognized Him and fell at His feet. This is the kind of intimacy small groups and one-on-one relationships create. With one word, Mary's grief lifted as she was called by name by her Rabboni, who is now her wonderful Savior. Jesus is a God of intimacy. He beckons us into intimacy, not only with Himself but also with the people around us.

How well do you know your neighbor?

In high school, I always loved watching people play those "know your partner" games that they would play at Valentine's banquets. I would quiz myself to see how much I knew about my partner and often found myself drawing a blank. As I look back, I realized I would pass off intimacy for a favorites test. Now that I'm married and realize intimacy includes emotional, spiritual, and physical closeness, I scoff at the superficiality of my relationships. It is easy to say you know someone. You know their birthday, their favorite color, where they work, and other facts. But it is something else entirely to say you are known by a person. Immediately a connotation of intimacy, vulnerability, and closeness is created.

Congregational worship allows us to know about one another. We get a quick life update before or after the service, but it does not allow us to delve deep into the issues that we all know others are facing. Behind the smiling face and handshake is someone who has lost purpose in their work, is struggling with how to be a good parent, feels deep shame for a current addiction, or is asking some really deep, faith-shattering questions for which they cannot seem to find answers. Small groups create an environment where we can no longer settle for "hi" and "bye" interactions. They create an atmosphere where people learn how to know God and be known by one another.

Spiritual intimacy and Tupperware

Spirituality, specifically our relationship with God, is meant to be shared. This fact does not discount the importance of private worship, where we connect with Jesus on a personal level, but it creates more accountability. We cannot share anything if we have not experienced it. In congregational worship, there are maybe two people who share their spiritual journey, the pastor and the worship leader. Sometimes it resonates with the needs of the people, and sometimes it misses its mark. Why? Because one person is trying to minister to dozens, hundreds, or more. When we gather in smaller groups and personally share what God is doing in our lives, we have eight to fifteen people sharing, and the odds of alignment are much higher.

Some of the most intimate spiritual moments I have shared were in a small group. During my time as a small-group leader at Southern Adventist University, I invited three girls from my small group to hang out and talk in my dorm room one Sabbath afternoon. What was supposed to be an informal get-together turned into a spontaneous Communion using Wheat Thins. We took my football-sized Tupperware bowls and washed each other's feet. As the girls tangibly felt God's presence in that space, they felt open enough to share their life stories. This was the first time they had shared their entire stories with others—before and through the tears and hugs. God was lifted up. From then on, we were spiritually tied to one another. We uplifted each other in prayer and continually reminded ourselves of where Jesus had brought us. Something powerful happens when the people of Christ come together and individually share how God has led in their life. Few moments can compare.

What's in it for me?
The idea of small groups may sound fine and dandy, but what is the real power in small groups? Isn't Sabbath School once a week enough? I do not want to discount the success (or lack thereof) of Sabbath School in your church and ministry. However, small groups provide three key components that are often lost in a Sabbath School class. Rather than focusing on getting through the week's lesson, small groups provide a chance for people to come and find community, accountability, and support for several areas of their life. Let's take a brief look at what each of these can mean.

1. Community. Johann Hari presented his research on addiction in a very impactful TED talk episode. He quotes, "The opposite of addiction is not sobriety. The opposite of addiction is connection."[1]

There are reasons why Solomon's counsel on finding good friends is so specific and Paul's pleas to dwell within community are so consistent. This is not to say every small group should be focused on addiction, but we can see the power that people loving and knowing other people holds. When a community of believers come together and are like-minded in mission and vulnerability, amazing things happen. The Holy Spirit descended upon a room of people who were submitted and dedicated to one cause together. As a group, they experienced God as they had never experienced Him before.

Those experiences are accessible to us as well. In small groups, we come together and realize we are all on a level playing field. We all need grace, and we are all messed up. We can find comfort in the fact that everyone is journeying, celebrate in our answered prayers, and build each other up in times of difficulty.

Evangelistically, small groups are a perfect segue into a Sabbath morning service. Your members can have a place to invite their neighbors, coworkers, clients, and others they know if those people feel uncomfortable walking into a church setting. It can be a lot more inviting to say, "Hey! I am having a bunch of people over this week. We have food, play some games, and we're reading this book together. You should totally come!" than perhaps inviting them to a two-hour church service. Once the guest feels comfortable enough, and they now know a small (or large) percentage of your church, inviting them to a Sabbath service isn't so foreign.

2. Accountability. I do not know what kind of church you have, but even churches with thirty members can run into issues of member inactivity. The larger you get, the more prevalent this becomes. The 15–20 percent carry the load for those remaining, and people abandon the responsibility of making their faith active. It is much easier to hide inactivity in a crowd of people at church than it is with a group of twelve.

If people in a small group are committed to growing spiritually and serving their community, an inactive member will stand out. Small groups, when done intentionally, create a space where people grow and serve. Each group can decide what spiritual muscle they want to strengthen, but the point is that stagnation is not an option. Discipleship comes as a result of this overflow. Once people take charge of their own faith and express it through action, they have to introduce others to Christ. You can no longer keep what God is doing to yourself. You are compelled to share it with those who don't know the kind of life they could live.

3. Support. Have you ever played Where's Waldo? Every dentist appointment, I would dedicate myself to finding this oddly striped man in a crowd full of people. It is meant to be difficult, and it often is. However, church shouldn't be a Where's Waldo experience, especially for guests. Finding Jesus and finding community shouldn't take years.

Small groups provide a tether point for churches, especially bigger ones, for all members to find community. People are no longer lost in the crowd, searching for something necessary for survival. Supportive and authentic relationships can be forged in small groups. It is also a great opportunity to provide guidance and support to those who are newly baptized. They do not have to figure out this whole "faith" thing on their own. Instead, they are given consistency and are led forward in their faith with people who were once at the same place.

Let's do this

I have briefly explained the principles of small groups—the outline sketch. Here are some necessary tools to start forming an idea in your mind for how to implement them in your church. I have several years of experience with small groups in a university setting. This allowed for a system where we had an overseeing chaplain, two paid student directors, and twenty paid LifeGroup coaches. This will look a bit different in a church setting, but it's still entirely possible.

You must first consider your "why." Why do you believe small groups are necessary at your church? How do they align with your mission and vision? What goals do you have for your small groups? What purpose do they serve? Would you be willing to support these groups with materials or a leader budget? You should have these conversations with God and your leadership team.

Once you have established your "why," you can move on to "who." Whom do you want to help lead out in this area? Think of the type of personalities you need. The format I recommend is to have someone who is in charge of small groups as a whole. This could be a paid position, stipend earner, or volunteer. This overseer provides accountability for the leaders of the small groups. He or she helps organize promotional events and provides mentorship for new and existing leaders. Members and guests can ask this person how to get involved with small groups, as either a leader or member. This person also keeps track of the different groups within the congregation and lives out of the overflow of a relationship with Jesus.

Once you have prayerfully filled that position, it is time to recruit leaders. Young and old, male or female, all should be welcomed to lead. We encourage each leader to collaborate with either another leader or a coleader so that the group does not become a burden. We also have found that in church settings, it works well for groups to set a limit on how long they run. You can decide with your team how long they should last, but we have seen anywhere from six to eight weeks at a time, two to three times a year. This schedule allows people to find new groups if they desire and gives the leaders time to refresh themselves spiritually. It also allows for variety in topics and provides opportunities for the small groups to study specific material for an upcoming event, such as an evangelistic series or a season of prayer.

Once your leaders are selected, you can allow them to decide the group's topic. It can focus on an issue pertinent to their lives or a book of the Bible they long to study. If possible, the church should provide materials to help support these groups.

The last step is promotion. Host a sign-up event. It can be as elaborate or as simple as you want. Have the leaders promote their groups and invite people to sign up for them. There can also be an online resource (whether it be a Google document or an addition on your church's website) where people can sign up. Video and text announcements might also be utilized. The point is to let people know exactly how to sign up for these small groups.

Conclusion

I pray for blessing and depth of community in your small-group project. I pray that you see lives changed and relationships formed. I pray that you see people come to Christ because they found a community. I pray that you, as a leader, find your own small group to invest in. I also pray that you experience the presence of God through worship and prayer in a group of people who are searching for God with their whole heart. Finally, I pray that an upper-room experience happens in your small-group ministry.

---

1. Johann Hari, "Everything You Think You Know About Addiction Is Wrong," TED video, 14:34, June 2015, https://www.ted.com/talks/johann_hari_everything_you_think_you _know_about_addiction_is_wrong/transcript?referrer=playlist-new_thoughts_on_addiction.

Vanessa Hairston is a seminary student at Andrews University with an undergraduate degree in education from Southern Adventist University. During her time at SAU, she worked in Campus Ministries as a LifeGroup coach and director. Her responsibilities included one-on-one mentorship, leading and coaching a small group, and discipleship.

Small Groups
Video Presentation (RT: 15:23)
Vanessa Hairston

CHAPTER 12

Identify Your Twelve People

Roy Ice

S o your church members are staring at you with that look on their faces. You know—the one that mumbles, "Pastor, what are you going to do to fill all of these empty seats in the church?" Perhaps they reminisce about the golden days when the place was packed. Can I set your mind at ease today? I know how you feel. You are maxed out. You are trying to preach your next home-run sermon, but the people are just sitting there in the pews, unmoved. Your stress level is rising alongside your workload, and you know there is no way you can work any harder. Your blood pressure is up, and your attendance is down. You would love to see your congregation activated. You want to experience more of a partnership with them instead of feeling as if you are all alone up there on the platform. So what do you do?

Can I share with you something that changed the perspectives of the membership at my church? I would like to show you how some of our attendees became invested disciples of Christ. I want you to see how doing *one thing* caused an atheist to insist on small-group Bible studies, a hairstylist to ask for spiritual advice, a very cranky neighbor to melt into a best friend, a local elder to invent a whole new paradigm for anointing services, my unchurched neighbor to ask for my testimony, a secular German film crew to interview me about the importance of spirituality, and a growing list of miraculous encounters that have come about simply by doing this *one thing*.

As pastors, what are we trying to build? Attendance? Community? Reputation? Involvement? What we all know in our heart of hearts is that none of these is either possible or sustainable unless we are building *disciples*. The preceding list of things that we desire is simply a list of the by-products of building and growing disciples.

So what is a disciple? We typically associate discipleship with involvement, but I strongly challenge that. I have many members who are involved, but they are not invested in a growing discipleship journey. In my opinion, you must make an investment (of time, talents, and/or money) to be on a discipleship journey. You must sacrifice something in order to experience the full risk of discipleship. It is one of the greatest oversights in the church culture of our time that members can consider themselves Christians for life but never categorize themselves as disciples. When Christ called His twelve, He did not say, "Take a look at your calendar and see if the first and third weekends look good for your schedule." No. He said, "Follow Me." Then He intentionally showed them how to do *one thing* over and over again, and in various contexts.

Laurie did one thing

That is what Laurie did. She did the one thing, and the Holy Spirit led her into one of the most memorable experiences of her life. She lives in West Virginia, but her sister, Carolyn, who lives here in Loma Linda, California, shared with her what we were doing. Laurie read and researched our materials and set out on her discipleship journey. Immediately, she felt the Holy Spirit impress her to start a small-group Bible study. There was just one problem. Laurie had never led one before. Nevertheless, God's moving was strong, and Laurie knew she had to follow through.

She followed our discipleship framework and prayed for God to help her make a list of twelve people to share God's love with. (You will read more about our discipleship framework in just a bit.) God stirred her heart deeply, and she began calling the people on her list to invite them to her home for Bible study. Everyone said yes, and she was getting more and more excited until she reached the bottom of her list. Individual number twelve was an atheist. Laurie paused. How could she call this atheist and invite her to a Bible study? She already knew what the reply would be. Why should she even call? But the Holy Spirit would not leave Laurie alone. Unable to do anything else, she called her. She braced herself for the certain rejection, but to her surprise, the atheist said, "Sure! That sounds fun."

If the story ended right there, it would be amazing enough, but it gets even better. After several weeks of conducting her small-group Bible study, Laurie had to travel to Tennessee for a wedding. She announced to the group that she would be out of town for two weeks and asked them to consider whether they wanted to continue after she returned, or if they thought it was a good time to take an extended break. To everyone's surprise, it was the *atheist* who protested and said, "We have to keep meeting. We can continue while you're gone!"

Shawna did one thing

Shawna did the *one thing* and filled out her list of twelve people on a Sunday. One of those twelve was her hairstylist. The next day, she went to her hair appointment. Up to that day, for seventeen years, Shawna had never had a spiritual conversation with her stylist. Nevertheless, because she did the *one thing*, as soon as the stylist placed the salon cape around Shawna, she asked, "You're a Christian, right? Would you mind if we talked about some spiritual things?" And for the first time, Shawna was able to share the good news of the gospel with her.

Don and Sandy did one thing

Don and Sandy have a beautiful house on a lake in Michigan. It is their summer getaway. There was just one major problem that kept this place from being their oasis of peace—their cranky, harassing neighbor. He would yell at Don and Sandy about their yard, their fence, even their very presence. Everything seemed to anger him. Don and Sandy did the *one thing*, placed this neighbor on their list, and prayed specifically for him. Sandy felt overwhelmingly impressed to bake some cookies and take some over to their neighbor. She followed the Spirit's inspiration and did just that.

When Sandy knocked on the door, the cranky neighbor answered it. He awkwardly accepted the plate of cookies and called for his wife to come to the door. After uncomfortable introductions, Sandy returned home wondering what would come of it. That evening, Don received a phone call from the cranky neighbor, inviting them to come over for dinner. In the course of the conversation, he asked if they had any food allergies. Don explained that they were vegetarians, and the neighbor exclaimed happily, "That's great! My wife is trying to be a vegetarian, and I'd like to work on some new recipes."

For two summers now, Don and Sandy have accepted their neighbor's *weekly* invitation to come over for dinner. Sandy shared with me in her last report that their once-cranky neighbor had just spent all day preparing a vegetarian Mediterranean soufflé for them. Now they laugh together, share stories, share life, and share their spiritual journey. All because Don and Sandy did the *one thing*.

Pam did one thing

Pam approached me in the church lobby, excited to share what was happening because she was following our new discipleship framework. She shared how God was using her with some of the people on her list. But then she began to look a little worried as she talked about one of her latest encounters. She said, "I sure hope I didn't do anything wrong here." Her face paled, and her eyes drooped a bit. "One of my twelve people has cancer. He goes to another church, and I tried calling one of his pastors to come over and perform an anointing for him. None of his pastors would call my friend back, so I thought, *Hmm. I'm a local elder, and James 5 says you can anoint if you're an elder, right?*"

I smiled and nodded.

"So I went to his house and anointed him. I sure hope I did it right. First, I put some olive oil on the back of his hands to symbolize that God could still work His will through him. Then I anointed his feet and prayed for God to lead him in this journey. I anointed his earlobes so that he might hear God's voice better. I anointed his lips, so he might speak God's will. I anointed his forehead so that he might have the mind of Christ. And finally, I anointed the top of his head, so that the Holy Spirit would fill him completely at the present time." She looked bashful. "Did I do it wrong?"

I was stunned. "Pam," I said with tears welling in my eyes, "I think *I've* been doing it wrong all these years! Would you mind if I borrowed this model for every anointing I do from now on?"

I do not know how you are feeling after reading this, but this experience knocked me to my knees. In a world where we have grown confident that we have learned everything we need to know to conduct successful ministry, God still has an infinite number of methods to share with us, to help us recalibrate to the changing world around us. And all of these experiences and more have happened in my church because we chose to do the *one thing*.

What is the *one thing*?

Let us take a look.

You are a follower of Christ, right? Why do you think He called *you* to follow Him? To save you? Of course! Perhaps because He loves you? Absolutely! However, as a *follower*, where do you think He is taking you? If the answer is that He is simply leading you back and forth between your couch and your pew in a kind of protective holding pattern until He comes to take you to heaven, that can become old and passionless really quick. It can also quickly morph what the church is producing—from making spiritual disciples into making the spiritually *disabled*.

Also, if we are following God with the intent of perfecting ourselves and paying homage to Him so that we might be one of the fortunate remnant who makes it to heaven, we will become narcissistic, exclusive, and disconnected from the world into which Christ commissioned us. So what does it mean to be a growing disciple, answering Christ's commission to "go and make disciples"? How did Jesus define it?

Jesus continually found Himself surrounded by people. He loved them all. Jesus loved the 5,000-plus who stayed past lunch to hear about the kingdom. He loved the 500 who followed as time permitted. Jesus loved the 120 who gathered in the upper room to pray for God's guidance at Pentecost. He loved the 72 who went door-to-door sharing the good news. But there was something about the 12 that brought out His deepest expression of love. These are the ones with whom He lived, walked, slept, taught, fished, healed, sailed, ate, and ultimately died. Christ invested the bulk of His time into these 12 disciples. They were diverse in their personalities, occupations, and religious beliefs. At least one, Matthew, was unchurched.

After living as an example, Jesus commissioned us to *go make disciples* as well (Matthew 28:18–20). In principle, He asked us to find twelve people to love—to invest our God-given love, our unquenchable hope for heaven, and our true concern for humanity. He asked us to intentionally replicate His teachings and His point of view but to do so with the distinct flavor of love (John 13:34, 35).

The call to disciple-making is a call to utilize your influence for God's kingdom. It is a proven rule that to have influence, you must have a relationship. If you have no relationship, you have no influence. So the simplest way to answer the Great Commission is *not* by going downtown and randomly calling people to "follow me!" No. God has already placed your disciples within your sphere of influence. They are members of your family, close friends, fellow church members, and your friends who do not even attend church. These are your disciples. Some of them just do not know it yet!

Influence is the *one thing* that has such a powerful impact on so many. It may sound simple, but it is definitely not simplistic. Perhaps you would like to learn more about this discipleship framework. If so, visit us at My12People .com.

The power of the one thing

The one thing changed our culture to its very core, so much so that when a secular film crew from Germany came through town, they noticed it. Three young adults, Sarah, Josh, and Victor, producing a television show for the

Health Channel in Germany, came into the church office on Thursday to get permission to film our worship services as part of the background footage for their series on the Blue Zones. I invited them to come over between our two worship services to the Bible Lab, one of our intergenerational Sabbath Schools, to experience a full vegetarian breakfast buffet. I did not expect them to stay for our Bible class, but in the midst of it, I noticed two of the guys filming me along with the rest of the crowd. Immediately afterward, the three Germans approached me and asked if they could interview me for their show. I chuckled and said that, although I have done much research on this topic, I did not really have anything of substance to add to the Blue Zone conversation.

Sarah quickly said, "No. We really want to interview you."

I asked, "Well, what questions do you think I might be able to answer?"

Sarah got a little teary-eyed and said, "I've traveled all over the world, and I've never been loved as much as I have experienced right here. From the moment I came into this place, people genuinely cared for me. They were so concerned that I had all of the papers and the welcome bag. They wanted to make sure I had a seat. They wanted to make sure I got something to eat and drink. One lady even invited me to sit with her. People were trying to make friends with me, and they do not even know me! I just have one question for you. Do you think that community has anything to do with longevity?"

I smiled. I could see what God was doing. "Sarah, I'd love to talk about this community on camera, but I have to ask you a question before we begin. I know that Germany is a very secular country, and I'm not sure how people will feel about what I'm about to say. Because, you see, I can't talk about community without also talking about spirituality. Are you OK with me doing that?"

"I don't care!" she blurted. "All I know is that I felt something here that I've never felt anywhere else! You can talk about whatever you want. The people in my country need to hear about this."

I said, "Well, then, let's roll the cameras!"

I do not know where Sarah, Josh, and Victor are this weekend, but I have one fervent prayer. Perhaps this Sabbath they will find themselves in your town. And perhaps they want to experience that *one thing* again.

So Sarah pulls out her smartphone and searches for a Seventh-day Adventist church nearby. She finds yours, and she puts your address into her GPS. When they set foot inside your church, what will their experience be? Will they confirm that our churches are the only places in the world where you can experience that *one thing*?

Roy Ice is the speaker/director of Faith for Today television broadcast ministries. He wrote The 12 People You Love while on his previous assignment as the pastor for Resource Development at the Loma Linda University Church. After field-testing his method of discipleship, it was made available so other churches can utilize this powerful approach.

The Twelve People You Love
Video Presentation (RT: 15:24)
Roy Ice

ACTION 5—PLANT

Multiply through
community-based
church planting.

Do Not Plant a Church for the Wrong Reason!

Jose Cortes Jr.

After preaching the Good News in Derbe and making many disciples, Paul and Barnabas returned to Lystra, Iconium, and Antioch of Pisidia, where they strengthened the believers. They encouraged them to continue in the faith, reminding them that we must suffer many hardships to enter the Kingdom of God. Paul and Barnabas also appointed elders in every church. With prayer and fasting, they turned the elders over to the care of the Lord, in whom they had put their trust.
—Acts 14:21–23, NLT

The Adventist Church across North America has placed a great amount of emphasis and resources in planting churches. More than nine hundred mission groups—that is what we call our new church plants—have been launched since 2015 in the United States, Canada, Bermuda, and the islands of Guam and Micronesia.

We plant churches because there are people in cities, towns, villages, and islands of North America who do not have access to the gospel through an Adventist church. If we want them to experience and hear the gospel through an Adventist church, we need to make the church accessible to them. One very effective way of doing this is by planting new mission groups in their midst.

Evangelism Action 5—Plant
Multiply through community-based church planting.
From 2015 to 2020, we surveyed and discussed evangelism with thousands of pastors, members, and church leaders. Our study resulted in six actions that could revolutionize mission and evangelism across North America. Seventy-eight percent ranked "plant" 7 or higher on a 1–10 scale. One reason for church planting is the simple principle that families that do not reproduce eventually disappear. If we want our beloved Adventist Church to be around

in North America till Jesus comes, community church planting needs to be a reality.

Although we believe that planting churches is essential to make the gospel accessible to people in every city, town, and island in our territory, we also believe that we must be very careful not to plant churches that misrepresent God and our church.

Reasons not to plant a church

If you are going to plant a church that does not love all sinners, does not care about what happens outside the walls of the building, and whose only purposes are to change people's religion and judge their behavior, please do not plant a church.

If you are going to plant a church because your present church is totally dysfunctional and the members are fighting and cannot get along, please do not plant a church and take all that dysfunctional DNA to the new church.

If you are going to plant a church right next door to a sister congregation that is already reaching the people and the demographics of that community to compete for their members and resources, please do not plant a church. The territory is too vast, and the number of unreached people too great, to be competing over a neighborhood that is already being reached. In church planting, collaboration is the name of the game, not competition.

Planting under any of these circumstances may be detrimental to our missional movement, hurt the reputation of our church, and above all, dishonor the God we serve. It is true that we really want to plant churches, yet we want to plant churches right.

Reasons to plant churches

Now that we have gone over some of the reasons *not* to plant a church, there are some reasons *to* plant that are important to consider.

Plant to make the gospel accessible. I would agree with other church-planting specialists that to make the gospel accessible through an Adventist church to each person in our community, we must have a church for every 25,000 inhabitants. This ratio means that in most of the larger cities across North America, we could have twice the number of churches that we have today without having to compete for territory or people.

Plant because we are the heart, eyes, hands, and feet of Jesus in our communities. Church planting is not just about having another place where we can hold worship services and corporately study the Sabbath School lesson. We plant churches because we desire to open up communities of compassion, places where people can experience the love of God and the compassion of Jesus in practical ways that are transformational to families and individuals. We are not interested in planting worship services but churches that love, serve with the community, equip new disciples, and worship regularly. A church that does not go beyond the four walls is not really a church; it is a club.

Plant to best position Adventism to reach new generations, residents, and people groups. Most older churches do not grow, but those that do grow gain the majority of their new members by transfers from other congregations. On the other hand, new churches generally baptize at a higher percentage than older churches and gain 60 to 80 percent of their new members from people who are not attending any church.

Although it is hard to swallow, older Adventist churches have a very hard time reaching millennials, Generation Z, and single mothers, who, together with their households, have become one of the largest people groups in North America. Older Adventist churches also struggle to reach the LGBTQ+ community and emerging immigrant groups. Planting new churches with different DNA can help to reach people whom our churches are not presently reaching.

Jesus did not preach an exclusive gospel. He founded an inclusive church. If our church can only reach people who think like us, dress like us, eat like us, smell like us, and worship like us, we will never be able to reach those who are different. Jesus came to save them too. We need to be more like Jesus.

Plant to help revitalize existing churches and to provide a natural environment for discipleship. One of the biggest pushbacks often used to reject church planting is, "Why plant more churches if the ones we have are dying?" Saying "we cannot plant a church because the ones we have are not doing well" is like saying "a family cannot have babies because grandma is sick." Churches, just like people, have a life span. Newborn babies keep the family going as grandparents age.

There should never be antagonism between church planting and church revitalization; they are both essential. When grandma is sick, we take her to the doctor and try to find a cure for her illness. However, if you stop having babies because grandma is aging, eventually, the family will be no more.

Church planting infuses new life and helps reset the life span of a plateauing or declining church. When an older church intentionally releases leaders and supports the birth of a new congregation, it rediscovers its purpose, and rallying around the new baby strengthens its health and missional resolve. As people are released for ministry in the new mission group, more people are required to step in and serve, thus creating an awesome opportunity for disciple making. Another great benefit of this process is that church plants, with mother churches, tend to grow stronger and faster than churches born without support.

Conclusion

Planting for the right reasons can be a blessing to the church and its surrounding communities. We have learned from the incarnational Jesus we follow that our churches should not be encased within four walls, filled with people who only talk to themselves and spiritualize everything while the surrounding world suffers. To resemble the Jesus we proclaim, we need churches that are a constant flow of blessings to their neighbors, classmates, colleagues, and those who simply walk the streets in need of hope. Jesus made life better and brought hope whenever He showed up. Our church plants and existing churches must reflect that if we expect to make a dent in our communities for the kingdom.

If you are going to plant a church centered in the salvation of God and the compassion of Jesus, a church that will be an agent of transformation in the community, please do not plant one church. For God's sake, plant thousands!

Please discuss this evangelism action with your church and how you can make it a reality in your setting.

CHAPTER 13

Plant Community Churches

Hyveth Williams

I won't be coming to church anymore," I declared to my pastor, Dr. Thros-tur Thordarson. I continued, "I feel the Lord has called me to do more than just sit in a church. I have been praying about this with one of my students, Heber Aviles, and I have decided to go to a section of Chicago and start knocking on doors. If you don't see me in church, it will be because I am out knocking on doors, praying with people, and seeing if I can find some who will study the Bible."

Pastor Throstur calmly responded, "Let's pray about this." When we finished praying, he said, "There is a little company I have in South Bend. They are not growing, and I'm thinking of disbanding them, but they meet in this beautiful church. Why don't you go and look at it before you go to Chicago? Just see what can come of it." The next Sabbath, I looked at the church, and I was just overwhelmed by the facilities, the location, and everything. It was just as if God was saying, "This is where I want you to minister."

Immediately, I contacted my friend, Heber, a seminarian, and we both prayed about the possibilities. We invited a few other individuals to join us, and the group grew eventually to twelve. We prayed and fasted together for a whole month, asking the Lord to reveal His will. The impression on all involved was that God wanted us to do something in South Bend, Indiana. Further affirmed in our goal and zeal, we became charter members and the executive team of "The Grace Place," as the church plant has been named.

We felt the Lord leading us to do a church plant with a community focus rather than simply another worship program for disgruntled or disenfran-chised Adventists. The thought was that if the community could be made healthy—spiritually, physically, and mentally—the church would grow and make a difference through innovative, creative, simple-acts-of-kindness evangelism. The plant was adopted by the South Bend First Seventh-day Adventist Church in the Indiana Conference, under the leadership of Dr. Thordarson.

Research of the city of South Bend revealed a population of 100,886 (2 percent of Indiana's 6.6 million residents). Of these, 66 percent claim some kind of religious affiliation (29 percent Methodists and 20 percent Catholics; Adventists were too small to make the list and may have been lumped with the 6 percent others). It was evident that there is a 44 percent unchurched population to reach with the gospel, so we enthusiastically selected an area for outreach that included about one-third of South Bend. We fasted and prayed for three months. In the last month, we spent the first week walking throughout the community in which we hoped to minister. We prayed for the people living there. We asked God to work in a mighty way to touch hearts and change lives.

The next week, we drove around the target community every day and prayed for it. We said, "Lord, we are claiming this community in Your name," according to Joshua 1:3. Each day of the third week, someone prayed in the church facility. We prayed that God would bless the work and not only change those who come to worship but also enable those ministering to be conduits of His love.

Following this, we fasted and prayed for ourselves and our leaders for a week. Then on Sabbath afternoons, we began visiting malls and shopping centers in the designated area. We gave out cards and prayed for and with people. We announced we were starting a community-based church plant on February 16, 2013. In addition to these efforts, 175 former Adventists living in the area were invited through personal visits, telephone calls, and written invitations to return to Christ and His church. Letters of apology were sent to each person. The letters, signed by me, said, "We apologize for whatever caused you to be disconnected from us. We want you back."

When visited, some people slammed their doors and said, "You are too late. Get lost!" However, a few accepted the invitation and came back. When the first church service began on February 16, 2013, ninety people were present, and at least fifty of them were from the community. Today, many have been baptized, and others have returned to the fellowship of the Seventh-day Adventist faith at The Grace Place, where an average of eighty people worship weekly.

Once worship services began, attendees were invited to share a Sabbath meal each week. Rather than having a potluck, a hospitality team prepared the food. The menu included two options: one with clean meats, such as chicken; the other was vegetarian. This menu allowed community visitors to sample vegetarian food and learn about it while still being able to eat something they were used to in well-prepared, balanced meals. A few months after her baptism, Janet Turner, the first community member to join, became a vegetarian, and the transformation of new members continues to amaze us all.

After the meal, those who are willing and able go out into the community to pray and invite people to worship at The Grace Place. They give out bread and other food as well as amenities, such as toothpaste, detergent, and light bulbs. Whatever we have, we give. Our gifts of love are changing lives. We have been told how different things are in the community since we started doing this.

When we first started, one man cursed us and slammed the door in our faces. "Don't bother me. I don't want to have anything to do with anybody!" he yelled.

Immediately we gathered on the front walk and prayed for him. Then we placed a bag of food near his door. As we were leaving, the man again opened the door. "We are from the Seventh-day Adventist Church, and we just wanted to pray with you and give you this bag of food," we told him.

"OK. You can pray for me," he responded.

During subsequent visits, we learned the man had lost both legs in the war in Afghanistan. He lived by himself and had no one to look after him, so members of the church began to check on him regularly. He has come a long way from cursing us to allowing us to pray with him, bring him things, and look after him. We see this connection drawing him closer to God and to others.

Being community-focused includes cleaning up the neighborhood. Sometimes these efforts involve snow removal. Sometimes they involve cleaning out a house where the people are just so depressed and overwhelmed that they cannot deal with it. Church members go in, scrub, throw out trash, and help organize the home. When we revamped a house in one neighborhood, the neighbors came around, looked, and asked, "Who are these people?" Curiosity drew them to the church and to the evangelistic meetings the church currently holds every summer. Many people have been baptized during these series.

While The Grace Place serves as a training lab for seminarians, the leadership team has found many ways to reach the community. Financial Peace seminars, diabetes seminars, and a health fair are just a few ways they have assisted residents. They also hosted a big Fourth of July party for the neighborhood. More than two hundred people came to enjoy free popcorn, a bounce house, and games for the children. Just for Kidz (J4K) is a monthly birthday program for parents having a hard time economically. Their kids are given a great party, taught Bible stories, and given birthday presents. At a July program, 107 children accompanied by 81 parents were treated to the best party imaginable. The Creative Café is another innovative community program reaching college and young professionals through the "Spoken Word," where many community people attend and share their poetry and songs about Jesus.

Our strategy does not focus on having a high worship service with the best singers, the best pianists, the best organists, and long offering appeals. We have a simple service with three parts—prayer, praise, and preaching. We do not pass around an offering plate. We have a box in front where worshipers, moved by the spirit, bring their tithes and offerings and deposit them. Generosity characterizes these gifts. Community residents see what the church is doing in the community, and they want to show their support by giving. Another unique aspect of The Grace Place is that transfers from other churches are not encouraged or even accepted unless the person has relocated to the community. While anyone may attend and are welcomed to the weekly worship experience, to be a member, one must be a returning Adventist or a new believer. This policy helps us see whether we are truly growing because, to me, transfers do not reflect church growth. The Word is getting out. The Grace Place is making a difference![1]

The why and how
Church planting is a biblical and strategic plan for soul winning and church growth, but it can be both exciting and frustrating. It is very exciting to start with a notion, even though inspired by the Holy Spirit, but nonetheless a notion that God has called you to take a risk with no safety net amid the quizzical looks and questions from other church members. It is frustrating because it is a minor financial commitment in the big evangelism budgets, especially for salaries and health insurance for the foot soldiers who are necessary to introduce the plans to anticipated members. It was exciting for me as a leader, who happens to be a woman who felt divinely called to such a mission because I was supported and mentored by professors and my pastor. It can be frustrating for a church planter, particularly a woman, who has no one to influence, mentor, sponsor, or open relationships and doors for them. As a result, for many, especially women who are called in a denomination like ours, where their presence is often unwelcome as elders or pastors, church planting can be a source of great disappointment.

Such obstacles, which stymie opportunities, contribute to a sobering reality. According to church growth experts, about one-third of church plants in North America do not survive. Perhaps more effective equipping and timely training of potential church planters is needed. They need to know how to train and provide mentors and members with the spirit and attitude of Barnabas (Acts 13:2). They must teach those who respond to God's call for this ministry or improve the skills required to start and lead thriving churches. They need to increase their knowledge about various types of church plants before taking on such a challenging prospect. Potential church planters need clear details about the opportunities and obstacles in church planting. They must also learn how to research and find consistent financial support for the long-term needs of a church plant.

For instance, consider five types of church plants:

1. *The parachute-drop model.* A parachute-drop church plant starts when a planter or family moves to a new location to start a church from scratch. The parachute-drop model needs a highly motivated and gifted leader. It can cost up to $10,000 annually in urban contexts and has a success rate of 25 percent.

2. *A regular church plant.* A mother church or organization provides the initial leadership and resources (people and finances) to start a daughter church in a new location, away from the parent church. The cost is generally low due to strong support, and the success rate is about 85 percent.

3. *Church split.* A plant from a church split that is caused by unresolved disagreements and hurt feelings in a congregation is not ideal because it hurts the witness of both churches to the reconciling power of God. Its survival depends on the shared vision of its members and on the length of time they are willing to work hard and contribute to its success.

4. *House- or cell-celebration model.* A house church plant is composed of small groups that meet in homes. Such groups may periodically network with other cells and may multiply using a relational house-church process. It is more effective in reaching unchurched people than other conventional models, but a major disadvantage is that it does not lend itself to children's ministry.

5. *Community-based church plant.* A church plant designed to primarily focus on the spiritual well-being of residents in a designated locale is

community based. Its emphasis is on discipleship and mission, serving Christ and others to achieve personal and communal spiritual growth. This is the model we chose to establish at The Grace Place (TGP).

Other than church plants started after an evangelistic series by the sponsoring or parent church, many Adventist church planters rely on small grants and stipends from local conferences for their financial support. They are unaware of the Entrepreneurial Church Planting (ECP) strategy, which we also use to support TGP. However, before sharing the why and how of our church plant, there are at least four models of ECP:

1. Business for saving the soul and planting churches, also known as the Tent-Making Movement, inspired by the mission of the apostle Paul, Aquila, and Priscilla. This method came into the spotlight in the 1980s when Christians used their professional business skills as a means to contact locals and eventually plant a church.[2]
2. The Business for Human Development model, which became popular in the latter half of the twentieth century when "the concept of *missio dei* began to gain acceptance."[3]
3. Business as Mission (BAM), "defined as business ventures led by Christians that are for-profit and are intentionally designated to be used as an instrument of God's mission to the world." This method is particularly popular in less-developed countries, which are "often hungry for business acumen and earning potential as well as jobs."[4]
4. Business for Holistic Transformation is based on the "view that Christian business in partnership with the community of faith can be a means to overcome materialism, individualism, and self-centeredness."[5]

When we made known our intention to establish a community-based church plant, we were often asked: "Why?" There are no major theological, ecclesiological, or sociological answers, but a simple "God wants to save me, and others, while so doing." Let me explain. Before accepting the call to teach at the Seventh-day Adventist Theological Seminary, I was senior pastor of a very active church in Loma Linda, California. Upon arrival at the seminary, I immediately joined a congregation, but after a year, I found myself becoming spiritually dry. Because I believe it is my responsibility to nurture my spirituality, I transferred to another congregation, only to find I had become a spectator who was often sleeping in church. It became clear to me that I was not only numbing my spirituality but also destroying my relationship with God because I was called to be an active participant in His mission to seek and save the lost. However, instead of finding suitable involvement, I resorted to complaints and the blame game until the Holy Spirit challenged me to do something about my situation, as described earlier. Thank God that so far, although there are at least five Adventist churches within a five-mile radius, The Grace Place has been like a pebble in a pond. Its influence and impact are rippling far beyond the borders of our local community.

Having never participated in a church plant, I needed to learn the "how to" of such a ministry. First, I fasted and prayed to ensure that this was a Holy Spirit directive and not an ego-driven vision to prop up my feelings and fear of getting lost in the spectator crowd. After being assured of the divine directive, I read far and wide about the advantages and opportunities. I immediately discovered the importance of recruiting volunteers and acquiring financial resources to fund the goal of planting a church. Fortunately, more than a decade ago, some friends joined me in establishing Hyveth Williams Ministries, a nonprofit organization headquartered in Riverside, California. This organization was and continues to be funded by my book sales, speaking fees, and donations. It was originally established to provide scholarships and promote evangelism. The time came when we had enough funds to be an entrepreneurial church plant, supporting other church planters and providing scholarships for students at a college in Kenya. We were making plans to send twelve volunteers to do evangelism in South Africa when the idea of a church plant was birthed. Hyveth Williams Ministries provided resources to launch The Grace Place[6] in South Bend, Indiana.

Here we now stand
We sing happily, "In Christ, the solid Rock, we stand"[7] because He has blessed us to be a growing church plant. In six years, we have baptized eighty new believers in Christ and reconciled several who have returned to our Adventist Church. Recently, most of our new members are families from our Just for Kidz monthly program. We have trained and equipped more than seventy seminarians, most of whom have been hired by various conferences across North America.

We are currently negotiating to purchase a church building so that we can be independent of the limitations that come with rented facilities. We are about to launch our boutique, where families from the community can receive new and pre-owned clothes. We serve a monthly meal to those who are homeless and provide them with warm clothes in winter. We visit our surrounding communities once a month in our Simple Acts of Kindness Evangelism (SAKE), where we distribute light bulbs, detergent, and bread. When we give away light bulbs, we remind recipients that Jesus is the Light of the world. With the detergent, we remind them that while this gift will wash their clothes clean, only Jesus can wash away our sin. Fresh bread helps impress upon them that where this bread will eventually run out, Jesus, the Bread of eternal life, will be with them forever—"ad infinitum."

Every Sabbath, we present a breakfast and Bible study for new believers and community folks, whose presence has increased exponentially. After services, our fellowship lunch gives us the opportunity to fellowship and share our stories.

---

1. Adapted from Betty Eaton, "The Grace Place Ministry Leads to Bible Studies and Baptisms," *Lake Union Herald* 107, no. 2 (February 2015): 25, 26, https://digitalcommons.andrews.edu/cgi/viewcontent.cgi?article=1051&context=luh-pubs.

2. Samuel Lee, "Can We Measure Success and Effectiveness of Entrepreneurial Church Planting?" *Evangelical Review of Theology* 40, no. 4 (2016): 330.

3. Lee, 331.

4. Lee, 332.

5. Lee, 333.

6. See The Grace Place website at https://www.thegraceplacesouthbend.org/.

7. Edward Mote, "My Hope Is Build on Nothing Less" (1834).

Pastor Hyveth Williams serves as director of the Doctor of Ministry program and professor of homiletics at the Seventh-day Adventist Theological Seminary. She holds a bachelor of arts in theology from Columbia Union College (now Washington Adventist University), a master of divinity from Andrews University, and a doctor of ministry from Boston University School of Theology. She served as the senior pastor of Campus Hill Church in Loma Linda, California and Boston Temple Seventh-day Adventist Church in Massachusetts; associate pastor at Sligo Church in Maryland; and a pastoral intern at All Nations Church in Berrien Springs, Michigan. She established The Grace Place in South Bend, Indiana.

A Pebble in the Pond
Video Presentation (RT: 17:41)
Hyveth Williams

CHAPTER 14

Lead Disciples in Planting Churches
That Plant Churches

Steve Leddy

Y ou have my life."
I was shocked at Jesse's response. "What?" is all I could stammer.
So he repeated his proclamation: "You have my life." This twenty-one-year-old young adult had just made the first of many commitments that others would make, though his declaration was certainly more striking.

I was part of a team just starting a new church targeting young adults. I had decided to try to plant this church, my fourth plant, differently. We would know what we were aiming for in making disciples before ever gathering a team. We first searched the Scriptures to figure out what these disciples are that Jesus commands us to make. What makes them true disciples? How do they live? How do they act? What do they do? And what do they believe?

Eventually, three themes became evident. Disciples are (1) mission-minded, (2) growth-seeking, and (3) community-embracing. It was our mandate to be unwavering in our commitment to these discipleship outcomes. We would not build a team, start a ministry, or make a decision that did not reflect these core discipleship principles. We wrote these up and had handouts ready to share with those we would interview, yes interview, to be part of the core team planting this new church.

This ministry model is what I had shared with the first person we interviewed, Jesse—a vision of a church that would be built around mission to the community. We would meet their needs, we would share the gospel in a language they understood, and we would be the living embodiment of Jesus' mission statement, "I came to seek and save the lost" (see Matthew 18:11; Luke 19:10). Being mission-minded meant we were creating a "next person" culture—we exist as a church for the next person coming in our doors who does not know Jesus.

Jesse learned that growth seekers are continually working to better themselves for the glory and mission of God, and they support others doing the same. He also learned that members are called to share the gift they received so others can accept eternal membership into God's family. We assured him that we would be journeying with him as he grew into a strong disciple, then he would be doing the same for others on their journey. Together, we would explore what excellence in all areas of life could do to bring God honor, and we would all grow as a spiritual family.

We talked about Jesus' prayer for His people to be unified. We were not starting a social club or a cool place to hang out; we were building an Acts-1-and-2-type loving family. "Brother" and "sister" would not be monikers lightly assigned—but lived as a reality. Loving one another would be the most powerful proof that God was working in this church, so we were going all in to become a united family. It was clear to us that going to church two hours a week would never lead to what Jesus wanted for us. We decided to gather in groups during the week, build friendships, and even seek ways to do our ministries as teammates.

Jesse shared with us how he had been raised in a larger church but never really was asked to get involved. His enthusiasm for church had almost hit rock bottom. Conversely, in his "real life," he was exceptionally creative and was a passionate, talented artist and filmmaker. At this point, I asked the question that prompted his amazing response, "Jesse, God has obviously blessed you with amazing gifts. You have heard us describe this different type of church God is leading us to start. Would you be willing to use your gifts to glorify God and help us build this church?"

"You have my life."

And this was no empty declaration. Jesse became a key member of our leadership team. Joined by his lovely new bride, they launched our youth programs and Sabbath School. They brought new people into our family. They started the most powerful prayer meeting I have ever attended. They led our campus outreach at the major university close by. Moreover, they became the launching pastors for another service in a different part of the city. God truly did get Jesse's life that day, and every day since.

Organic multiplication

This story illustrates God's method of organic multiplication—one life transformed into His likeness that then helps others as the Holy Spirit leads their transformation. Jesus spent years investing in the lives of His small band of disciples. As they grew, they were sent out to towns and villages to prepare these for His arrival. Eventually, filled by the promised Spirit, they led the new church. And those churches established more churches.

- Members share with future members.
- Disciples make future disciples.
- Leaders develop future leaders.
- Churches plant future churches.

Leaders of today's church should understand these principles and be ready to equip their members to make them a reality. The entire process works as a collaborative system. If leaders ignore one of these principles, the entire system slows to a halt. Have you ever wondered why the large majority of the churches in the North American Division have plateaued or are shrinking? It is either because we have abandoned one or more of these organic multiplication principles or because we have tried to replace it with one of the thousands of human-made programs claiming to be the answer to all our problems.

The practical stuff

If we understand the principles of building God's church through organic multiplication, how do we apply them practically in our local congregations? To be honest, there is no one pathway to achieve organic multiplication. Principles point us in the right direction, but how we travel there is usually unique. When you try to copy the exact methods another church used, you can find you will need to make numerous adjustments and revisions because it does not work the same way in your context. That being said, having an example can spur ideas and give us a starting place, so we will share some of our processes.

I woke up early the other morning and took a step on the floor. Immediately, I knew something was wrong. I quickly guessed that what I had just stepped in was from the newest member of our family: a rescued chihuahua. When I turned on the light, there was vomit and diarrhea on the floor and even the wall. Hercules had caught a doggie bug and had made a huge mess while we slept. I took him outside, cleaned him up, and then came into our room to see my wife scrubbing the evidence of his illness.

We had met Hercules at a shelter on Long Island, where we learned he had been abused and starved. He had numerous broken ribs in the past; his teeth were mostly gone as well as part of his lower jaw; he had experienced heart failure, liver issues, kidney disease, and the list went on. They put him in a small room with us, and he growled more like a lion than a tiny dog. When we decided to adopt him, the shelter's director cried. No one had wanted this sick, angry little guy. He said they were planning to put him down, and he was so thrilled this tiny bundle of fury would finally get to go to someone's home.

Why did we not leave him there? Why would someone want to deal with all of Hercules's health issues? Why did we not yell at him for making such a huge mess in our room? The word that explains this is *love*. My wife fell in love with him the second she saw him. It took me quite a bit longer—at least thirty seconds. Love transformed us; we did not see a sick, angry beast. We saw a cute, three-pound little dog that needed our love. His transformation has been nothing short of phenomenal. Hercules now loves people and has the sweetest temperament.

This story illustrates how Jesus loves all people. We make messes, are angry and crabby, and have all been infected with the sickness of sin. Nevertheless, His love for us is not predicated on our worthiness. He loved us before we ever knew about or accepted His love. That transformational love is imparted to us so that we can see the world with His loving eyes. There are people around us heading to Christ-less graves; this breaks His heart, and it should break ours as well. As leaders, we must prepare our members to love our neighbors, build relationships with them, and invite them to share in the gift of grace offered them.

We use a combination of approaches to both help their love for the lost grow and teach them how to lead people to the Cross. We do short surveys with no clipboards (do not be that person) to determine the community's greatest needs. Then we find creative approaches to meet those needs. We work on each member's personal testimony. Strategically sharing how God has impacted your life is very powerful. People can argue against the validity or your interpretation of the Bible, but they cannot deny your experiences. We show them how to recognize what different spiritual realities people may be living with and how to approach each unique situation. Moreover, we collectively get involved in our community in a variety of ways.

You cannot become like Jesus if you do not serve others, period. Jesus is the perfect Servant. Discipleship is the process of becoming closer to Christ, walking with Him on His mission to this world, and being transformed into His likeness. Churches that stop helping members grow at baptism actually hurt the work of Christ. They develop a culture of consumerism and complacency that affects most new people joining their congregation. This culture is not the life Jesus calls us to lead. If a member is too busy to serve Christ, they have made an idol of the things they have chosen to put before God's calling. Does that sound harsh? I believe that if Jesus walked into many of our churches today, He would be braiding His whip to chase the pew-potatoes off their comfortable fannies. I can hear Him saying, "I have called you to be My Body in this world, but you have made My Church a den of spectators!"

No one grows into a strong disciple overnight. Some leaders seem to think that transformation is instantaneous. It is almost as if they are telling new converts, "I have been following and growing in my Christian walk for thirty years, and you should be just like me immediately." This attitude chases people out of the church, discourages them terribly, or creates legalists. Instead, we need to have a clear process we use to help people grow. We need to understand that the growth rate is unique for each new believer. If we do not have a clear system designed to help new believers grow, then their stagnation is largely our fault. However, when we have the foresight to help them, we will see people grow into powerful disciples of Christ.

When Jesus poured Himself into His disciples, what did He expect they would do? He was preparing them to lead His church. Strong disciples are leaders. Sadly, some are now thinking, *Every time I try to get people to lead a ministry, they either decline or make excuses.* That is because we have not first helped them to develop as leaders. When we create job descriptions for our various ministry positions, they all have the same thing listed as their number one requirement: "Train a replacement to know and do what you know and do." Systems only help if you have leaders creating and actualizing them. Plans are a dime a dozen; effective implementation and execution are the true vehicles of action.

Led to be a leader

I became an Adventist in my midteens. I was blessed to be baptized into a church outside of Denver, Colorado, that invested in the growth of their members, including the youth. They made me a Pathfinder junior director and allowed me to be creative in the small leadership roles it afforded. I helped in the youth department, sang in a youth choir, played volleyball and basketball in the gym, did plays that toured to other churches and a prison, and was involved in a variety of other ways. However, the church leaders did not just try to make sure we had a fun community; they pushed us to lead as well.

I am the only Adventist in my family. Since my family did not go to my church, I rode my bicycle twenty miles round trip from my home. If it was raining, I was still expected to show up to participate in the ministries I had volunteered for. I was made a junior deacon, which included getting the keys to open or close the church when my turn came in the rotation. Even when it snowed, I rode my bike to unlock the church and turn on the lights and heat well before everyone arrived. The leaders leading me and the members training me did not expect less from me than they were doing, nor did they expect to hear excuses from me.

When my fiancé (now my beautiful wife) started attending a university on the other side of the country, I followed her. My family did not have the resources for me to attend, so I rented a cheap apartment and found a part-time job at a Pizza Hut close by. After showing me the basics of making pizzas, the managers had a meeting to attend. The managers told me to clean the kitchen if the business slowed down. When they came out of their meeting, I thought I had done something wrong when I heard, "What happened to the kitchen?" Then I realized they were pleased with how clean it was. For some reason, this made them think I would be a good shift-manager—you know, the lowest limb on the management tree.

Shortly after my promotion, I was summoned to a training event for all the other new Pizza Hut shift managers in the region. During the few days we spent together, it became apparent to the trainers I was doing well, so they chose me to lead a team. Then they asked the five team leaders to speak for five to seven minutes on a powerful topic: "Why is making pizza important?" When I spoke, a few tears were shed. At the end of the training, the class voted me for some award like, most impactful—I forget the exact title. My wife likes to say it was the "Biggest Mouth Award." But after the training, the owner of the restaurants asked her, "How does Steve know so much about leading? He is so young." Her reply is the reason for this illustration. She replied, "Our church taught him how to lead."

When we invest in our people and help them lead in their ministries, their jobs, their homes, and in any area of life, then they will impact the world around them, and their influence will grow. I was soon made a manager of a store. I used the creative leadership principles I had been shown at church to grow sales dramatically. I invested in my workers the way that my church had invested in me. Within two years, we set an annual national sales growth record, and numerous restaurants in our chain were led by managers I had trained. Then they promoted me to area manager, one of three in the company. This was the highest position I could have without being an owner. One of my main roles was to plant new Pizza Huts. Twenty-two years as a church planter and God prepared me as a youth in a disciple-making church and at a Pizza Hut franchise. Wow, God is so awesome!

Leaders must have places to lead

If we assume your church is all in on leaders developing future leaders, you will find there is a major obstacle. If your church has ten strong leaders and each commit to train one additional strong leader each year, at the end of two years, how many strong leaders would you have? Twenty, of course. Now, assume they do the same. At the end of two years, you will have twenty leaders raising up twenty more leaders. If this happens the third year, your forty leaders will be replicating themselves, and now you have eighty strong leaders. Can you see the problem? Most churches do not have roles for even twenty strong leaders, let alone eighty. So how can we create opportunities for people to lead in God's work?

When I planted my first church, I had no idea what I was doing. However, I had an amazing senior pastor, Doug Bing, who understood the power of multiplication. We took a huge percentage of his congregation across town to plant a church, including the children's department leaders. I was afraid to take so many from key roles, so I asked him whether this was something we should rethink. He said God was leading this and told me to take everyone who felt called to go. Within months of launching the church plant, every role was filled at the sending church. People who had previously not been involved in a ministry took most of the positions. They were now growing as leaders. Moreover, those who went to the plant greatly expanded their involvement as well. Church plants naturally produce disciples and leaders in God's work. When we do not multiply churches, we create a barrier for multiplication in other vital areas.

Conclusion

When Jesus ascended to heaven, He gave His new church these instructions: "You shall receive power when the Holy Spirit has come upon you; and you shall be witnesses to Me in Jerusalem, and in all Judea and Samaria, and to the end of the earth" (Acts 1:8, NKJV). The Holy Spirit came as promised, thousands were added that day, and many more thousands continued pouring in led by God into His family. Did His disciples follow Jesus' instructions and start moving this message into Judaea, Samaria, and throughout the world? Reading Acts, we see that they did not. They stayed right in Jerusalem. Maybe they said to themselves, "We have so many new people we need to stay here and tend these sheep." Or maybe they started feeling the thrill of being megachurch pastors and forgot their call to spread the good news everywhere. Whatever the case, God had to bring persecution on His church to get them to follow the plan He gave them. "At that time a great persecution arose against the church *which was at Jerusalem*; and they were all scattered throughout the regions of Judea and Samaria, except the apostles" (Acts 8:1, NKJV).

We need to be the multipliers God calls us to be: each member sharing their faith and adding new members, disciples mentoring and making new disciples, leaders identifying and building new leaders, and churches expanding their missional reach by planting new churches.[1]

---

1. Excerpts from Steve Leddy's book, *Church X Impacts Their Community: How to Creatively Reach Your Communities for Jesus*, were adapted to create this chapter.

Steve and Melissa Leddy have worked together in ministry for twenty-three years. Steve is the director for Evangelism and Church Planting in the Potomac Conference. He founded the Church Planting and Adventist Leadership School (CPALS), which provides training for young adults with no ministry experience or education; the Church Planting Institute (CPI) for pastors and lay leaders; and Allies in Mission (AIM), which is a mission-effectiveness and discipleship-training program for new and existing churches.

Make Disciples
Video Presentation (RT: 25:37)
Steve Leddy

CHAPTER 15

Evangelize in the Context of a Multiplying Church Plant

Sergio Quevedo

Reflecting Jesus' character

When we started planting churches, we had something very clear in our minds: we wanted to plant churches that reflected the character of Jesus. We intended that these church members would be people who did everything they could to imitate Him—people who hoped to be like their Master!

In ancient times, a disciple would leave his family behind to sit at the feet of his master (Luke 10:39; Acts 22:3). The act of sitting at the feet of a master was symbolic of someone dedicated to taking in as much as they could to imitate him later. If I were to explain discipleship to my eight-year-old daughter, I would say this: "Honey, a disciple of Jesus is someone who lives their life having only one goal: to be just like Jesus." This description seems way too simple to be everything we need to know about discipleship; however, that is exactly what Jesus tells us to do in John 20:21. "As the Father has sent Me, I also send you" (NKJV). In this sentence, He is saying: "Imitate Me, be like Me, do what My Father and I are doing." We look at how Jesus responded to being sent, and we do the same!

The church, as a whole, has not totally ignored this concept. When imitating the Master, it has simply chosen to focus on two aspects—Jesus' communion with the Father and His sinless life. There is no doubt that God gives the Holy Spirit to His church to transform it from the inside out, helping members overcome sinful behavior, making them more like Jesus in purity, and giving them victory over temptation. However, that is not all Jesus did. If it were, He could have isolated Himself in the wilderness, away from everything else, to keep Himself uncontaminated by sin. There is another whole side to the story that we tend to forget! Jesus mingled with people as one who desired their good; He befriended them, ministered to their needs, gained their trust, and ultimately invited them to follow Him.[1]

Paul says, "Be imitators of me, just as I also am of Christ" (1 Corinthians 11:1, NET). John also tells us, "Whoever says he abides in him ought to walk in the same way in which he walked" (1 John 2:6, ESV). As Jesus invited people to follow, or imitate, Him, He meant the whole package, not only the "spiritual" aspect. He invited people to imitate Him, denying themselves and building a reputation of being disciples of Jesus by the self-sacrificing manner in which they loved one another (John 13:35).

Jesus practiced three categories of activities while here on earth: (1) He mingled and befriended (*belonging*). (2) He *blessed*, and He communed with the Father, (3) while helping others to do the same (*belief*).[2]

Belonging

One of the best ways to mingle with people and befriend them is by eating with them. This fact might explain why Jesus ate with people all the time. I do not mean this in a negative way, but people did accuse Him of being a glutton and a drunkard. Oh, and a friend of thieves, tax collectors, and sinners too! The last part of the accusation found in Matthew 11:19 is actually true—He did include tax collectors and sinners in His circle of friends. Jesus was not a glutton or a drunkard, however. He was assumed guilty by association because He did a whole lot of hanging out with those people. If I am to be sent as the Father sent Jesus (John 20:21), then I am called to do the same things and can expect the same accusations and reputation Jesus had.

In the Gospel of Luke alone, we see more than twelve saving encounters Jesus had with people while sharing food. For a Gospel with twenty-four chapters, we could say Jesus was eating with someone every other chapter! Even just before His death, the last time He and the disciples were together was over Passover dinner (Matthew 26). At their first encounters after the Resurrection, both in Emmaus (Luke 24:28–30) and in the upper room (verses 41–43), food was involved. When He appeared to them by the Sea of Galilee, He prepared breakfast for them (John 21). Jesus promised the disciples He would not eat of the bread and the wine until they are together in the kingdom of heaven (Luke 22:16; Matthew 26:29)—so guess what we will do at our first time hanging out with Jesus in heaven? *Eat!* If Jesus practiced social inclusion through hanging out with people over food, that means we are called to do the same as imitators of Jesus.

Creating a routine or rhythm is essential for this to work. We are naturally inclined to keep to ourselves, and after a hard day of work, the last thing many of us want to do is to have people over or hang out somewhere. We are not suggesting you add another activity to burden your already very busy life. The goal is to align our lives to the mission. For example, we all eat at least a few times a day; on average, twenty-one meals a week—if you eat three times a day. We are not suggesting that you add meals to your schedule, but that you give some of the meals you are already planning to Jesus. So let us say you have twenty-one meals in a week, and you decide to give three away. This decision means that you will pray for God to open the opportunity for you to have meals with three people during that week.

Another way of doing this is throwing parties regularly, such as getting some neighbors and friends to come over for potluck on a weeknight. We are talking about a social gathering around food—that is a party. If you can make that a regular meetup, that is even better. These parties are a place for social inclusion and not a trap to get more Bible studies. So please, just be a friend; enjoy developing genuine relationships with people. This concept is great news, as we get to be Christians and be pleasant people at the same time! As you do these things, following the example of Jesus, you will stick out from the crowd and make people curious.

Blessing

As we look to the example of Jesus, it is quite clear that He dedicated a great part of His ministry to restoring, healing, and serving—another word we could use for those activities is *blessing*. In the covenant made with Abraham, the Lord tells him he would be blessed in blessing others—through Abraham, all of the families of the earth were supposed to be blessed (Genesis 12:1–3). Peter reminds the church of this covenant and says that it is still valid. First Peter 3:9 says *you are to bless* "because to this you were called so that you may inherit a blessing" (NIV). He says the church is called to be a blessing! The covenant was not only for the physical children of Abraham but to all who become heirs through Jesus Christ. That means every blessing we receive should be turned into a blessing for somebody else. This concept alters the notion that receiving blessings is the easiest thing in the world—blessings come with a burden attached to them; to bless others. We are blessed to bless.

At One Connection Church (the church we planted), we created small accountability groups that meet regularly to read the Bible, pray, and tell each other about our experiences blessing our neighbors. We committed to each other that we were going to bless three people every week. Of course, this needs to be a prayerful effort—the Lord is the one creating the opportunities. As we mingle with people in our neighborhood, school, or workplace, we get to befriend them and learn their needs. As we find out what the needs are, we try to minister to them. Some needs are more obvious than others, but whatever they are, we must be sensitive to the voice of the Holy Spirit in order to recognize them. We begin by praying that God will put someone in our path for us to bless that day. Blessing others thus becomes intentional. This is one prayer you can be sure He will answer.

One Thursday evening, we were at the church building where we gather. The band rehearsed while some others set up sound and other things. As we were getting ready for the gathering on Saturday, the guitar player called me over and asked me, "Do you have an Allen wrench? My guitar has a tuning lock, and I can't tune it without this wrench." I looked around but could find no Allen wrench in sight. I thought I could just go across the street—since we were downtown—and buy one for less than five dollars at the hardware store. But on second thought, I decided this would be too easy and efficient. I could use this opportunity to get to know some of the neighbors in that community because we were new there and had not really connected with many of the neighbors. I said a little prayer, "Lord put someone in my path whom I can be a blessing to."

As I left the church building, I saw a lady and asked if she would have an Allen key or wrench. She shrugged her shoulders and told me she had no idea what that was. I kept walking up the street until I saw another lady who had a similar reaction when I asked. Across the street, I saw a woman with three small children taking her groceries into her apartment building. She was very stressed, even yelling at her little one when he dropped a gallon of chocolate milk. I felt sorry for her situation and thought I would help—that is when she yelled at me, "What do you want?" I just repeated the same speech about the Allen wrench I needed to tune the guitar. She said, "I have no idea what that is, but go into this other building and look for a guy named Sean. He is a musician and might be able to help you." By that time, she had gained control of her chaotic situation, so I thanked her and walked away.

I opened the front door of Sean's building, which was unlocked. I later found out that the door is never unlocked. I started looking for Sean's name in the directory on the mailboxes, but they all showed last names, and I only knew his first name. So I walked up the first flight of stairs and decided to just knock on a door. As I knocked on the door, a man came and, without opening it, shouted, "Who is this?" I said, "Well, I'm looking for Sean, a musician. I'm from the church down the street, and I'm looking for a little tool we need to fix one of our guitars."

When I mentioned the word *guitars*, he opened the door in a hurry and said: "Hi, I'm Sean!"

I said, "Hey brother, how are you? Sorry to bother you, but would you have an Allen key by any chance?"

Sean said, "Allen key . . . hmmm . . . I don't think I do, but I do have a guitar, and I could play for you."

I almost took a step back, but I said: "OK, we can try that."

"You said church, right?"

I said, "Yes, just down the street."

"Well . . . I have been drinking this afternoon, up until you showed up at my door. Do you think that is going to be a problem?"

I started thinking, *Is that going to be a problem?* Everything I had learned growing up told me I should stay away from him and, more important, keep him away from holy people in a holy place. However, there was only one voice I needed to hear at that moment, and that was the voice of the Holy Spirit: *What would Jesus tell him right now?*

That was enough for me. I said, "Sean, let's go! You're playing with us tonight!"

He smiled and said, "Come inside for a few moments while I get some things ready to go."

I went inside, and he turned and locked the door with a huge deadbolt. I cringed and thought, *Oh man, I might be in trouble here.* We walked over to his kitchen, and I saw a bag of tobacco on the table next to the bottle of beer he had been drinking. He was rolling the tobacco in cigarette papers so he could smoke for a fraction of the price of a carton at the store. He wanted to get a few more "ciggies" for the trip, and I sat down with him as he rolled them in a little device.

Sean started to share some things about himself, and we were having a wonderful conversation. A few minutes into it, I just looked around and could not help thinking to myself, *What am I doing here? I went out to get a little tool, and now I am sitting at a table, in an apartment with liquor all around, rolling cigarettes with someone I do not even know!*

Somehow, as dangerous as it felt, I realized that this was exactly the kind of situation Jesus found Himself in time after time. He was accused of hanging out with and making friends of sinners and thieves (tax collectors).

We went down to the church, and as we walked in, the people looked confused. Not because of Sean but because they knew I had left to get a tool and I walked in with a human being—and still no tool!

I introduced Sean to the group: "Hey guys, this is Sean, and he's joining us tonight. Get ready; he plays a mean guitar!" He had demonstrated a few of his skills at the apartment, and it was truly extraordinary.

They immediately embraced him and made him feel comfortable. He played with the band that night, and it was simply astounding. The band was struggling before he came; when he played, all of a sudden, everything came together.

At the end of rehearsal, they spent another couple of hours with him. Nothing special—just mingling as people who desire this guy's good and want to become friends with him.

That night after we left, Sean sent me a text message saying, "Hey Serge, tonight was nothing short of amazing. I felt wanted and loved for the first time in many, many years. Playing music was just a bonus. Sean."

This message really moved me as I saw that the church was fulfilling its purpose. Everything about Sean was different from what you would normally see in church. Nevertheless, he was accepted and loved as one of our own. Two days later, on Saturday, Sean played with the band. He was overjoyed, and so were we. By the way, this time, he had not been drinking—even though no one told him to show up sober.

The following week I took him out for a bite, and he shared some of his life story. He did not have an easy time growing up. He had suffered so much abuse that it affected him in many areas of his life, even to the present day. He also shared how his parents and sister had given up on him and that he had been spending Thanksgiving and Christmas by himself for almost two decades. When I heard that, it broke my heart. I could not contain the tears, and we both cried together. I told him, "From now on, you will spend Thanksgiving and Christmas with my family and me."

If we are the good news of the kingdom, and if we are to bring the kingdom of heaven to earth, it is inconceivable that someone around us would spend a holiday alone because they are lonely or have been deserted. If in the kingdom to come, no one will be alone during special dates, then we are called to replicate that reality around us in the present. That day, by God's grace, Sean had a small glimpse of what the kingdom of heaven is like—and he liked it.

The church adopted Sean, and now several people continue to make the kingdom tangible to him. He is no longer a lonely person. He has gotten to know God on a personal level through small groups and just hanging out with the church community. He was discipled over time—to do for others what had been done for him. He slowly cut down the drinking and the smoking—even though no one told him to. Everyone could see the Holy Spirit working in his life. Many amazing things happened in his life, and I could fill many pages writing about them. However, I am going to end with this: Sean asked to be baptized, and we baptized him. All the glory and honor is to God, who never gives up on people and loves people no matter where they are. As we blessed, the Lord added to His church.

Belief

Communion with the Father is to the soul what oxygen is to the lungs. Serious time in prayer and the study of God's Word is the only way any of this will make any sense. Ultimately, Jesus wants a personal relationship with His children, and we must have that experience if we are to make any difference as missionaries in His church. Jesus spent a lot of time with the Father (Mark 1:35), and He states that this is one of the characteristics of a true disciple: "If you abide in My word, you are My disciples indeed" (John 8:31, NKJV). Jesus does not play around when it comes to having a strong connection with Him. He says, "I am the vine; you are the branches. If you remain in me and I in you, you will bear much fruit; apart from me you can do nothing" (John 15:5, NIV). There is nothing we can do without knowing Jesus personally.

We know that Jesus befriended people (social inclusion); He ministered to their needs (blessing), and then He finally invited them to follow Him (communion). If we do the first two genuinely and authentically, we can be sure He will create the opportunities for us to take the third step of connecting people with Him. The problem, many times, is that we use the first two steps (social inclusion and blessing) as a means to an end—the end is getting people to join the church. Again, our goal should never be to grow the church, as this is Christ's job (Matthew 16:18). Our job is to make disciples the way Jesus did (John 20:21; Matthew 28:19, 20). Disciple making goes beyond leading people to commune with Jesus. It is helping them imitate Jesus in every way. Jesus spent much time mingling and blessing, and so should we.

Sharing comes from personal experience. When asked, one of the most effective ways to do this is to share your story and then share the story of Jesus. The question usually comes at a personal level, so you would not go into theology right away. However, the question is related to your experience with God. We should "give a reason for the *hope* that lives within *us*." This is not to say we are limited to one way of answering. Again, the Holy Spirit will lead, and in whatever way the opportunity presents itself, we will adapt and act accordingly.

Helping people make a transition happens in several ways. It starts in a personal relationship with us as His disciples. Then, development and growth continue through small groups, fellowship, worship gatherings, prayer groups, and other elements. As disciples, we talk at length about our small groups and our missional communities. They are a powerful tool in developing new, Word-abiding disciples.

Conclusion

To imitate Christ, we must look at all the aspects of His ministry. We just looked at a three-pronged approach that Jesus used while here on earth. He mingled and befriended people—belonging (horizontal); He ministered to their needs—blessing (horizontal); He communed with the Father and called others to make that connection through Him—belief (vertical). A disciple will practice all three aspects, not just one or two. We usually honor someone who spends much time in prayer and the study of the Scriptures with the title of "spiritual person." There is no problem with that, as long as this person also practices the other two activities. A spiritual person is someone who dedicates his or her life to all three forms of ministry—a true imitator of Jesus Christ.

---

1. See Ellen G. White, *The Ministry of Healing* (Mountain View, CA: Pacific Press®, 1942), 143.

2. See Hugh Halter and Matt Smay, *The Tangible Kingdom: Creating Incarnational Community* (San Francisco: Jossey-Bass, 2008), loc. 447, 448, Kindle.

Sergio Quevedo is the Church Planting coordinator for the Southern New England Conference, where he develops pastors and lay leaders for the work of church-planting and disciple-making. He has pastored and planted churches in the secular New England area of North America. Quevedo also works in partnership with the North American Division and the General Conference of Seventh-day Adventists to catalyze new church planting movements in North America and around the world.

Be the Good News
Video Presentation (RT: 20:37)
Sergio Quevedo

CHAPTER 16

Plant Churches With Volunteer Lay Pastors

Matt and Amy Stockdale

My name is Matt Stockdale, and I am an attorney in North Carolina. I am also an adjunct professor at a local university. And I am a church planter. Three jobs. Listed in order of income but not necessarily in order of their sense of achievement.

How it all started

I first felt called to plant a church back around 2012. I was an elder in my local church and taught the young-adult Sabbath School class. I recognized the need for a church where young-adults and those disconnected from a traditional church would be welcomed and allowed to be actively involved in ministry. At the time, I owned and operated a law firm, making a comfortable six-figure income. Success came with a price—namely, working six days and averaging eighty working hours a week. Quite frankly, I did not have time to plant a church, and as a result, I resisted the call for about a year.

As often happens, the calling to plant a church never subsided but actually increased—I am beyond thankful for that. In 2013, I made the difficult decision to shut down my law firm and accept a position as an assistant district attorney. Then, as a state employee, I had the benefit of a forty-hour workweek despite the 50 percent decrease in salary. The transition was not easy but was made possible due to my amazing wife, Amy, who supported my calling.

With the additional time, I, along with a dedicated team, started the process of planting what would become Triad Adventist Fellowship (TAF). We met weekly for nine months before ever holding a public worship service. As a core group, we became family and developed a church model from the ground up. The only prerequisites to our church were the Adventist doctrines;

everything else was debatable. "Sacred cows" were slain along the way.

During that time, I read all I could find on church planting. I discovered that the recommendation is to have a church for every 25,000 in population. The Piedmont Triad area of North Carolina has 1.6 million people. When I did the math, I was shocked to discover that we needed about sixty-four churches in an area that had fewer than twenty churches—less than one-third the amount needed to become a movement.

Volunteer lay pastor—what's that?

I was encouraged to learn that my local conference fully supported church planting. What I first found to be a bit odd, but have since found to be necessary, was that my local conference required church planting to be lay-led. This requirement is due to the shortage of full-time pastors. The situation is complicated even more by the rising average age of full-time pastors. Planting the number of churches needed to become a movement is impossible without using volunteer lay pastors.

Triad Adventist Fellowship, which began with twelve dedicated lay members, launched public services in July 2014. We grew faster than we ever imagined. We currently have 160 members, and our average attendance revolves around 180. I never expected to be leading a church of this size. Our membership is diverse, both ethnically and in age—it is like seeing a glimpse of heaven here on earth. We are actively preparing to plant another church that will specifically target college students and young professionals. We cannot wait to see what God has in store for this next chapter of our journey.

The North American Division has developed a Volunteer Lay Pastor (VLP) program now being implemented by many of our conferences. This program provides the necessary tools and training needed to advance the cause of planting lay-led churches in our division. Since we (VLPs) have not been seminary trained, we need help tackling many of the challenges of leading a church. In my opinion, it is also important to reimburse the VLPs for some of their expenses incurred while leading a local church. Being a VLP is certainly not a means of getting rich—far from it—but it is important to feel valued and appreciated for the many hours of hard work invested in advancing God's mission.

The VLP program is not a path to full-time employment within the denomination. It is merely using dedicated, trained individuals to reach those far from God. It is a return to the biblical model of ministry. Full-time pastors should never fear the VLP program. It will not replace the valuable work done by full-time pastors. Our mission is best served when we collaborate and use our collective resources and abilities to further the work in our division. Together, and only together, we can make Adventism a movement again.

OK—now what?

The journey as a volunteer lay pastor has been both challenging and rewarding. I cannot express the joy associated with this journey. Seeing people decide to follow Christ and then following them on that journey through baptism to active ministry to others warms my heart and reminds me why I do this.

Ministering to the "least of these" in our community, with no strings attached, has restored and strengthened my faith in humanity. Our area was ranked second in the United States for food insecurity in 2013. People did not know where their next meal would come from. When I first saw that statistic, it blew my mind. How could a little area like ours be worse than the big cities? But it was. We, as a church community, decided that we could not sit back and act as if nothing was wrong when hunger was so prevalent in our community.

We started small. We started donating to a local food bank. That first step never ceased, and to date, we have donated over sixty thousand meals to the hungry in our community. The method we use is pretty remarkable. Every time a person checks in on Facebook at our church, we make a donation to a local charity. Facebook check-in can be a conversation starter. We encourage our members to say something like, "My church donates to a local charity for every check-in. Ask me about it, or come and join us." Each member has Facebook friends who know nothing about Adventism and may not even have a relationship with God. This check-in can and does start conversations, which have led to visits to our church and conversions to Christ.

However, it goes further than that. When we feed the hungry, without expecting anything in return, we are following Christ's method of evangelism. We are meeting people where they are and then meeting their needs. Once we build a relationship with them, we can then invite them to our church, and they will feel comfortable coming because they know we have met their needs and love them regardless of the mistakes in their life.

After taking that first step, we found other ways to combat hunger in our community. We currently provide breakfast every Friday morning to the homeless and hungry at a local park in our city. Rain, sun, or snow—our dedicated team is there every Friday morning. When we saw the needs of the homeless, we decided to start giving out basic toiletries and clothing to our neighbors in need. We provide an evening meal to about a hundred people at a local homeless shelter once a month. The workers at the shelter have told us that our church is different from any other group that provides meals. Most groups simply hand the people a plate of food as they come into the shelter. We do it differently. We ask each person to take a seat, and then our members treat the person like a guest at a restaurant. We bring them a drink and a plate of food and then a dessert. We treat them like we would want to be treated at a nice restaurant. We also ensure that we always have plenty of food so that anyone who might want seconds or even a to-go box will never be turned away hungry. Simple, and yet it can make a profound impact.

Our first year, we thought it would be good to get the names of some needy families and provide a food box at Thanksgiving. We provided fifty families with boxes. Afterward, we were happy, but I could not help but think that there was something else we could do—something we were missing. We talked about it and finally figured it out. First, why do we only do this once a year? Second, a box of food is great, but a relationship is better. As a result, we changed the program. We started to do food boxes at least quarterly, and then we assigned families to members within our church. A member takes the food box to the same family over and over again—and a relationship forms. They get to know the family and their specific needs.

We also actively participate in helping out other worthwhile nonprofit organizations. There is no need to reinvent the wheel if there are already perfectly good programs in place, meeting the needs of the least of these. We have partnered with a local orphanage to help abused and neglected children find their forever families. Some of our young adults hosted a free Christmas concert where we took up a love offering to raise money for the children. We have worked with a local nonprofit food pantry to help raise funds and collect food to deliver to area shut-ins and persons struggling to find low-cost medications. We also took gift cards and purchased and pumped gas for our least-fortunate neighborhoods when devastating tornadoes unexpectedly hit our community. Being out in our community shows our neighbors that we care about them and that we want to help them, whether it is financially, physically, or spiritually. Our community knows who we are, and they ask us for assistance in times of need.

I cannot leave this section without mentioning the actions of one of our young adults. One Sabbath morning, as she was driving to church, she saw some individuals standing at an intersection asking for food. She turned her car around and invited them to our church since we provide breakfast and lunch every week. These individuals have been regular attenders at church and lunch for several months now. We know them by name and ask about them when they are not at church. They know that we accept them as they are, and we welcome them with open arms. All because of the willing heart of a young adult.

Many other projects have been started and continue to impact our community. All of these projects can be achieved only through the dedication of volunteers who simply want to introduce people to their best Friend, Jesus.

It is not all gravy

Up to this point, it might seem as though being a VLP is the greatest position one could ever achieve. The reality is, it is not all gravy. There has been a fair share of challenges along the way.

There has been a dual challenge to being a VLP. On the one hand, some members expect you to fulfill all the roles of a full-time pastor, including always being available. I have two other jobs that I must maintain to pay the bills. Consequently, I am often not available during business hours. It is also extremely difficult to find extra time to visit members—both in their homes and if they happen to be in the hospital. On the other hand, some members refuse to recognize that you are functioning in a pastoral role at your church. Some even try to undermine your leadership in ways that ultimately damage the congregation.

Although my local conference has generally been supportive of VLPs, there have been minor issues, such as not being included in emails sent to all of the other local area pastors. Or scheduling meetings with the local pastors during the business day, when a VLP is likely at work and unable to attend. Conferences should do everything they can to encourage younger members to become VLPs. At the training I have attended, I have noticed that many of the VLPs are retirees. Based on time commitments, this makes sense, but we also need younger members to plant and lead churches that are likely to reach their peers. I hope that conferences will make extra efforts to recruit younger members into their existing VLP programs.

On a personal level, the sacrifices made to become a VLP have been difficult. Taking a 50 percent pay cut has put financial strains on my family. My overall workload has not decreased. I used to work eighty hours a week at my law firm. I now work eighty hours a week between my jobs and my church. This workload is not healthy and could be a major hindrance to someone choosing to become a VLP. It can also lead to burnout. The additional time away from my wife has, at times, put a strain on our marriage.

There are many wonderful aspects to being a volunteer lay pastor, but as you can see, there are also serious challenges. A healthy and balanced lifestyle is paramount to ensure success—both current and future—as a volunteer lay pastor.

A VLP's wife's opinion

Planting a church takes patience, time, energy, effort, and a relentless commitment to sharing Jesus' love with everyone you meet. You will get discouraged and feel like you are progressing one foot—but losing three or four. You will be overwhelmed. You will wonder why you do it. Nevertheless, you know why you do it. It is for the people who need to hear about the love of Jesus. However, it is also for people like me. I am a third-generation Seventh-day Adventist on both sides of my family. My parents met at Andrews University. And, yes, I found myself sitting in my home church, thinking, *Where are all the people with whom I went to church school? I know they are still living in the area, so to what church are they going? Or are they going to church at all?* I knew that my home church was not the kind of church that I wanted to attend. I went there because I was expected to, not because it was the style of worship that I preferred. I wore a suit every day for work, so I did not want to dress up on one of the two days when I did not have to wear a suit. I have nothing against "Amazing Grace" or any of the old standard hymns, but more modern praise music is what speaks to my heart. I realized that I did not look forward to going to church, so why would any of the people with whom I went to school? We had done the same style of worship all of our lives, and it was not meeting my needs anymore.

I was always active in church and had taught and then led out in the Kindergarten class at my home church from the time I was in the tenth grade until I left the state to go to law school. I think that is what truly kept me going to church. I had made a commitment to those kids, and I was going to live up to it. However, I wanted more. I wanted to do more to help my community. Moreover, I wanted to be around an entirely authentic group of people who would do anything to show others in our community the love of Jesus. I wanted to help the least of these.

I want to encourage you if you are considering starting a church plant that you can do this even if you are an introvert, like my husband, Matt. Being a VLP is not like being an MVP. The most valuable people in our church are the ones who stay behind the scenes, quietly running the children's Sabbath School programs, emptying trash, putting out tithe envelopes, and cooking the weekly meals. Why are these the most valuable people? Well, they help ease the burden of the VLP. I would like to emphasize the importance of everyone helping out. Church planting is a group effort because one VLP cannot do everything on his or her own.

The wife of a VLP makes sacrifices. In my case, it was not only monetarily, when my husband's salary was cut drastically and I had to start living with a stricter budget. It is, more important, the time that I miss being able to spend with my spouse. I am not sure that anyone ever tells you, "Hey, we've got this great opportunity for you! You're going to have all the responsibilities of being a pastor but none of the official recognition and none of the pay. We won't let you baptize people you lead to Christ, but the good news is you will spend countless hours dealing with the bureaucracy that is the church system." So remember you *do* make a difference in people's lives. Your work is important, and your work is critical to those who have never heard about the love of Jesus!

The bottom line is that no one else is going to step up and do the work. You have to do it, and you can do it. God promises to be with those who draw near to Him. So draw near to your core team members, and draw close to God. He will protect you and sustain you and guide you with His loving arms if you will just listen to the call He is placing on your life. Follow it, and obey God.

Back to the beginning
My name is Matt Stockdale, and I am an attorney in North Carolina. I am also an adjunct professor at a local university. And I am a church planter. Three jobs. Listed in order of income but *not* in order of their sense of achievement. Being a volunteer lay pastor provides me with the greatest sense of achievement. I encourage each of you to support the VLP program and encourage your members to accept the challenge of being a missionary for Christ.

Matt and Amy Stockdale are practicing attorneys. Their lives are busy but not busy enough to ignore a call from God to plant a church in 2014. The result of that call is Triad Adventist Fellowship in Greensboro, North Carolina. While continuing to practice law, Matt serves as a volunteer lay pastor.

Triad Adventist Fellowship
Video Presentation (RT: 22:20)
Matt and Amy Stockdale

ACTION 6—REVITALIZE

Multiply through diagnosing and implementing growth strategies for plateaued and declining churches.

My First Church Revitalization Experience

Jose Cortes Jr.

"I know all the things you do, and that you have a reputation for be-
ing alive—but you are dead. Wake up! Strengthen what little remains,
for even what is left is almost dead. I find that your actions do not
meet the requirements of my God."
—Revelation 3:1, 2, NLT

You are going to be the associate pastor for the Arlington, Falls Church, and Manassas Spanish Churches in Northern Virginia. Although you will serve all three, your main responsibility will be at the Manassas Spanish Church." Those were the marching orders from my Hispanic coordinator, Pastor Ruben Ramos, right after my return from the Seventh-day Adventist Theological Seminary.

On my first Sabbath, there were thirty-eight people in attendance. It was summer, and the people were very loving with me; yet the service, and the atmosphere in general, felt cold. I preached the best sermon I had but did not hear a whole lot of amens or affirmations. I could not tell what it was, but something was wrong.

It is unfortunate yet true that many pastors in North America will, at some point in their ministry, pastor a church that has either plateaued, is declining, or in some cases, is dying. There are stories of church growth, church planting, and church multiplication across our territory, but there are also plenty of anecdotes, backed up by data, that sadly reveal the fragility of church life.

The life span of a church in North America is similar to the life span of human beings, somewhere between eighty to one hundred years. While we recognize some churches will plateau, decline, and someday die, we must be clear that there are also churches that manage to live, thrive, and reproduce way beyond their life expectancy. Just as we love to see our grandparents and parents live long and stay healthy, we want to see churches stay healthy, stay relevant to the mission, and serve their communities for many years.

After that first service, I asked to meet with the four elders whom I had just been introduced to for the first time earlier that morning. I asked them two questions.

First, I asked, "How are you doing?"

"We are tired; the church is not doing well; many have stopped attending; we are dwindling; if we do not do something we are not going anywhere," was the collective answer to my first question.

"What can we do to make it better?" was my second question.

"Pastor, we need to have Communion—we are divided, we are discouraged. Could we plan a Communion?"

We agreed we would have Communion the following Sabbath. Since most members had now gone home, we organized as a team and divided responsibilities to contact the members and invite them for Communion the next Sabbath. This was our first team-building session. Carlos Alfaro, the head elder of the church, a very humble man, stayed back with me after the meeting. With tears in his eyes, he said: "Pastor Jose, this is a tough church. We have been through a lot. You are a young man, but I am here to work together."

Afterward, he invited me to his house for a delicious lunch prepared by his wife.

Eight months later, the Potomac Conference leadership asked me to serve as the senior pastor at an English-speaking church. On the farewell Sabbath, my last day in Manassas, more than 120 people attended, 40 new people had been baptized, and about 40 more had been reclaimed during the preceding eight months. What had happened? The church had been revitalized! I just did not know it at the time. Perhaps revitalization was not a thing back then.

Quickly, let me share with you the lessons I learned from my first church revitalization experience:

Prayer works

On my third Sabbath, I preached about prayer. I told the church that I needed people to pray for me and with me. We gave out a card and asked those who would commit to praying intentionally for the next three months to fill it out. I got seventeen cards back. Seventeen committed prayer partners began praying. Mercedes Rodriguez, one of the elders, started a prayer group in the church.

Visitation works

During our second elders' meeting, we discussed that elders do not exist just for the sake of performing platform duty. They can be an extension of the pastor in the church and community at large. At our second meeting, our elders' team became the pastoral team. In the following Sabbath's bulletin, the pastoral team, pastor and elders, was listed in the bulletin with contact info. We also talked about the role of deacons and deaconesses, looked at their biblical role, and agreed that visiting our active and missing members was vital.

The pastoral team met, looked through the church directory, and assigned each elder to care for a group of families and individuals. Visiting each one of our families and members began right away. I went out with a different elder every Tuesday, Wednesday (morning and afternoon), and Thursday to visit. Each elder committed an evening a week for visitation. We learned not to visit alone, so when they were not visiting with me, they always took a deacon and deaconess with them. We started with the active members, and once we finished visiting the active members, we visited the missing members.

Our visits were very simple. We tried not to stay for more than twenty-five minutes, although we often noticed they wanted us to stay longer, and just about everyone offered us food. During the visit, we asked, (1) How are you and your family doing? (2) How can the church help you? (3) What can the church do better? (4) How would you like to get engaged in some type of ministry? After that, we read one Bible verse, prayed for the family or individual, and left.

At times, arranging a visit was challenging due to the busy schedule of the working families in the church. Most had more than one job, plus children to care for, but we still offered the visit. Very few did not take us up on our offer. The majority of the visits took place in the homes in the evenings between five and nine o'clock, with exceptions of mornings and early afternoons in cases of retired, older, and unemployed members. Some visits happened at the workplace during a break, at a restaurant over a meal, in the hospital for those who were not well, and at the church, before or after a service.

Visitation provided the opportunity to meet and make friends with family members, spouses, and children who did not attend our church. It also created a great bond with the elders and deacons. All of a sudden, we were on the same page and had a cohesive missional team! As word spread that we visited and prayed with people, community neighbors began contacting us to request visits in the homes of non-Adventists and in hospitals to talk with people and pray for the sick. As we found out about needs, members in the church offered some assistance and support to those in need. Although we were not wealthy and were unable to take care of all the needs, people around us could sense our love.

Teaching works

On Wednesday nights, we began a study series on the parables of Jesus and their practical application to our daily lives. A grace-oriented sermon series was introduced for Sabbaths. I preached on the anchors of our faith—our beliefs and how they were given by God to bless our lives. On the back of the church bulletin, initially produced weekly by me, there was a detachable connect card, which, among other things, included a space for sermon topic suggestions. I paid attention to a large number of them—not all, but many.

Prioritizing children and youth works

We requested help from a few members who seemed to have a gift to expand our children's programs and launched a small group for youth. We held it in a home on Friday nights, and it was led by the two active young adults we had, Jose Luis and Rosalia. We planned outings on Saturday nights. The local Pizza Hut and bowling allies got some business from us during those eight months. Our small-group Bible study grew to around thirty attendees. Youth and young adults began participating in worship services. We did take a few hits for using a screen and an overhead projector from a nearby independent ministry school. However, now that our church was growing, our members were engaged, and our youth were coming back, no one had much time for criticism.

The Potomac Conference organized a Youth Congress at Camp Blue Ridge. The cost was forty-five dollars per person. Our church board met and voted to pay the whole amount for every young person and their friends who wanted to attend the congress. Thirty-five, including some who had never been to church before, signed up. The total attendance for the event was 310. Our little church had 35 of those 310! Our youth felt special and very motivated, and so did their young-adult leaders. We invested about $2,000 in sponsoring our youth to attend that congress. It was so worth it! They loved it, and you should have heard the parents talk about how much they enjoyed being part of a church that loved their kids.

**Inviting people to make decisions to accept Jesus
and join the church works**

The first baptism came a few weeks after my first Sabbath. A couple, Lazaro and Sandra, decided to be baptized. We baptized them on a Wednesday night in the church's basement. It is interesting to see how the baptism of one in-spires others. Whenever people made decisions to accept Jesus and join our church, we baptized them. We did not wait to have evangelistic meetings or special days to baptize people who made decisions. Every decision was celebrated, taken seriously, followed up, and acted upon. During my last month there, we had a special Easter Week of Evangelism. We spent $200 at Office Depot copying the flyers. We asked members to bring their family, friends, and colleagues. I preached every night about the Passion Week, Jesus' death, and His resurrection. I made appeals every night, and on the last Sabbath, we baptized sixteen people in one shot.

That is what we did. God blessed, and the church was revitalized!

Now, I am not so naive as to suggest this is the silver bullet for church revitalization. This was just what worked for me in that particular situation. Perhaps some of these lessons, if contextualized to your setting, could bless your church revitalization journey.

Evangelism Action 6—Revitalize

Multiply through diagnosing and implementing growth strategies for plateaued and declining churches.

From 2015 to 2020, we surveyed and discussed evangelism with thousands of pastors, members, and church leaders. Our study resulted in six actions that could revolutionize mission and evangelism across North America. During the last three years, we have worked on "revitalize." Nearly everyone we vetted this action with agrees—we have declining and plateauing churches, and we would love to see them become growing and, ultimately, multiplying churches.

Please discuss this evangelism action with your church and how you can make it a reality in your setting.

CHAPTER 17

Grow Young Adventists: Generations Thriving Together

Tara VinCross, D. P. Harris, Jessie A. López,
Steve McHan, Sue Smith, and Nick Snell

Edited by A. Allan Martin

Church-board member Kristi was part of a team from the San Marcos Seventh-day Adventist Church that attended the Growing Together Summit held in San Antonio, Texas. Her team, as well as intergenerational teams from more than twenty other churches, embraced core commitments that can make a church a great place to grow. One of these commitments, "Keychain Leadership," talks about entrusting young people with access and authority to influence their local church.

Kristi and her team were pretty fired up about what they had learned and were eager to share it with their congregation. At the summit, they made intentional plans to help their whole church love the next generations better. Kristi had some ideas as to how to apply the core commitments as early as the next Sabbath.

It would be great to have young people help with greeting Sabbath mornings, Kristi thought, given that she was already volunteering in that area.

When church leaders give opportunities for the next generations to be involved, it helps young people form a sense of identity, belonging, and purpose within their church.

"The young people were so excited to greet, some of them headed out into the parking lot to welcome people and hand out compliments," lauded Kristi. "It was incredible."

Enter five-year-old Sarah

Adult greeters Vilma and Kristi invited Sarah to join their greeting team one Sabbath morning, and the glow on Sarah's little face could be matched only in the responsive warmth of those she welcomed to church. Sarah was so thrilled to be a greeter at church that following the greeting experience, she promptly marched into Pastor Josue's office and asked if there was anything else she could do to help in the church. Sarah was fired up. Vilma, Kristi, and Pastor Josue could not have been more delighted.

When young people love their church, embracing responsibility and leadership, the *whole* church benefits—all generations. Growing Young Adventists (#GYA) is about drawing the next generations into the vitality of church life and discovering not only the vibrancy of intergenerational relationships but, moreover, finding Jesus at the center of it all.

Growing Young Adventists is a learning journey for local churches and leaders, teaching them how to help build faith communities that will not only survive but also thrive in the years ahead. This intergenerational movement nurtures relationship building and cultural transformation. It embraces young people and benefits all generations in the Adventist Church.

Sarah is one of tens of thousands of young people who can be invited, even at a very early age, to serve and minister in their local church. Sure, it will take additional effort and require building trust in youth and young adults. Nevertheless, if Sarah is any indication, it is well worth it.[1]

Sparked by the North American Division but taking root in the unions, conferences, and local churches across our territory, #GYA endeavors to cheer, support, and provide resources to congregations who desire the vitality of our young people and the great relationships they bring. #GYA is here to

- *cheer*. We celebrate great Adventist people in warm churches who are building wholesome, authentic relationships with young people. *#GYA loves to tell growing young stories.*
- *support*. We nurture Adventist churches and organizations that desire to grow young with the collective experience and shared wisdom of ministry leaders, point people, and passionate volunteers. *#GYA is here to help.*
- *provide resources*. We equip growing young communities by supplying mentoring, materials, and ministry training that help Adventists love the next generations better. *#GYA has stuff to share.*

Growing Young Adventists is based on the groundbreaking research by the Fuller Youth Institute in its book *Growing Young: Six Essential Strategies to Help Young People Discover and Love Your Church*. The book profiles more than 250 innovative churches that are engaging fifteen- to twenty-nine-year-olds. These churches—reflecting the denominational spectrum, varying in size, and located all over the country—are growing spiritually, emotionally, in mission work, and numerically.[2]

Authors Kara Powell, Jake Mulder, and Brad Griffin show that reaching young people does not boil down to hyper-entertaining programs, trendy locations, or other attractions. What matters most are relationships, empathy, community, and Jesus.

Essential strategies for growing young

The authors outline six strategies essential to engaging young people:

1. *Unlock keychain leadership.* Keychain leaders entrust others with access and authority. They empower all generations, including teens and emerging adults, with their own metaphorical "set of keys" to help influence and shape the direction of the church.
2. *Empathize with today's young people.* Empathizing means "*feeling with* young people" as they grapple with existential questions of identity, belonging, and purpose; as they experience "systemic abandonment" because of divorce and the self-absorbed adults around them; and as they act out a desire for connection through social media.
3. *Take Jesus' message seriously.* The authors were struck by how, in the churches studied, "Jesus reigns over poor theology, and his words ring true for young sojourners hungry for life-giving direction." One young interviewee said, "The goal for our church is not really effectiveness with young people, but serving and following Jesus. And young people like me are attracted to churches that want to do that."
4. *Fuel a warm community.* "Warm is the new cool" in these congregations, where authenticity triumphs over worship style or a multitude of programs. Young people who participated in the research praised their churches for "warm" attributes, such as welcoming, belonging, accepting, hospitable, and caring.
5. *Prioritize young people (and families) everywhere.* Churches in the study revealed a disproportionate prioritization of young people—an impulse that, rather than excluding older generations, breathed life

into the entire congregation. As one pastor put it, "Everyone rises when you focus on young people." Involving young people in every ministry has allowed these churches to thrive with authenticity and intergenerational relationships.

6. *Be the best neighbors.* The authors found that in churches growing young, the community accepts the difficult task of offering young people a thoughtful path to neighboring well. They provide opportunities for teens and emerging adults to serve others, pursue social justice, find their calling, interact with popular culture, and respond to heated cultural issues.

The authors debunk myths about the changes that churches need to make to grow young; offer guidance on creating a plan for change; and include helpful sidebars, case studies, and other tools.[3]

Reviewing *Growing Young* for *Ministry* magazine, Dr. Bill Bossert offered, "Although none of those factors listed were of surprise to me, it was how the authors pulled each of those core commitments into a revolving wheel where each core commitment fed into the next that did. Churches that were growing young had incorporated into their church DNA those core commitments. Their research also showed that before any one of those core commitments, opportunity for the local church to opt out, and head back towards growing old, could and does happen."[4]

Although Dr. Bossert was not surprised by the findings, he found the resources and discussion, chapter after chapter of each of the commitments, relevant and helpful for implementation in his local church.

"After a chapter devoted to each of those six core commitments, the authors devote a chapter to how to implement all six into the local context of my church," Bossert continued. "I found their process of change important and of great value to me. I have asked my main leadership team to read the book, and then we will meet to discuss how we can establish these six core commitments into our church missional ministry."[5]

Growing Young Adventists is an opportunity to encourage our church to love the next generations well. We want to cheer, support, and provide resources to congregations who desire the vitality of our young people and the great relationships they bring. Let us make the Seventh-day Adventist Church the best place for not only young people but all generations to grow!

Throughout our division, churches are thriving as they live out a transformational culture in which generations are taking to heart #GYA. A wonderful example is Azure Hills Church, which is among the vibrant churches where generations are growing . . . together.

Azure Hills Church is a diverse, multigenerational Seventh-day Adventist community devoted to their mission to "live by God's grace, grow in love, and be a voice of hope."[6] Located in Grand Terrace, California, in the Southeastern California Conference, they have more than 2,300 members and a passion to disciple people of all ages, meet community needs, and worship our incredible God. Their #GYA story is best told by their church leaders.

GROWING TOGETHER IN LOVE

Unlock Keychain Leadership
Pastor Tara VinCross

Empathize With Today's Young People
Elder Steve McHan

Take Jesus' Message Seriously
Pastor Nick Snell

Fuel a Warm Community
Pastor Jessie A. López

Prioritizing Young People and Young Families Everywhere
Elder D. P. Harris

Be the Best Neighbors
Elder Sue Smith

Unlock keychain leadership
Tara J. VinCross, DMin, senior pastor, Azure Hills Church

> *Keychain leaders entrust others with access and authority, and empower all generations including teens and emerging adults with their own metaphorical "set of keys" to help influence and shape the direction of the church.*[7]

I was fifteen years old when I was baptized into Jesus and joined the Seventh-day Adventist Church. I was sixteen years old when I was asked to serve on the church board in my local church, invited to colead a Bible study group, and given keys to the campus-ministries office on my academy campus. I was not treated as a young person to be managed but as a leader to partner with. This trust changed the way that I viewed myself and influenced how I engage in ministry today.

According to Powell, Mulder, and Griffin, "keychain leaders" know what "keys" they have on their keychain—that is, the power and access they have— and are intentional about how they empower others, including teenagers and emerging adults, with their own set of keys.[8] "Keychain leaders model a posture of giving away access and authority."[9]

Now, after twenty years of pastoral ministry in three states, I can attest that this is a guiding leadership principle in my ministry: entrusting and empowering all ages in the body of Christ to do the work God has called us to do. Intergenerational partnerships make us stronger, healthier, and truer to our mission, even if in the process, it can take more time and investment.

Azure Hills Church (AHC) is a Seventh-day Adventist congregation in Southern California that was established fifty-five years ago. One of the principles that we continue to live into is the value of empowering leadership. Here are some of the ways we do this in our local church context.

Intergenerational Leadership Teams. Nearly every ministry team at AHC includes representation from all generations, including our church board, elders, deacons, media, and worship. One of our elders loves to tell a story from years ago when a guest confronted him because the teenager who passed him the offering plate wore a badge that said *Deacon.* He said, "Don't you mean *junior deacon?*" Our elder's response was swift: "We don't distinguish on the basis of age, but on the gifts of God." Involving younger generations in these key areas of leadership changes our ministry for the better.

Culture. In the AHC environment, it is expected that everyone has something to offer, from the youngest among us to the oldest and all in between. For the past three years, we have hosted a ministry fair in our fellowship hall. Like a job fair, each ministry has a table and can share how people can get involved. Rather than the nominating committee exclusively selecting who is involved in ministry, people are encouraged to take a spiritual gifts discovery workshop and to seek ways to get involved in ministry based on those gifts. Young people know that they are needed and wanted—but not only that, they can see a clear path to step into ministry.

Partnership. As was discovered in the research for the book *Growing Young,* our emerging adults expressed a greater desire for more connection with older generations. One of our long-standing adult Sabbath Schools heard their heart and decided to provide food each week, reaching out to bring breakfast and friendship. The message was clear and warmly received: "You're not just a group meeting in a room of the church. You are part of us, and we need you." Many of these emerging adult leaders have keys to the church, and they are involved in leadership positions. At the same time, they continue to need the investment of mature leaders who show up and express care.

Unlocking keychain leadership is about making space for the next generations alongside current leaders. It is about discovering greater clarity in our mission through the tension and challenge of engaging our faith with those younger or older than we are. It is about deepening our trust in God as we share authentically with each other. It is about imagining what is not yet in our churches and our communities as we bring young people into leadership. It is about stepping forward to dream, implement, and discover all that God has planned for this next chapter in the history of the church.

Empathize with today's young people
Steve McHan, MDiv, elder, Azure Hills Church

> Empathize with today's young people means "feeling with young people" as they grapple with existential questions of identity, belonging, and purpose; as they experience "systemic abandonment" due to divorce and the self-absorbed adults around them; and as they act out a desire for connection through social media.[10]

When we moved to Southern California in 2014, my wife and I were looking for a church family to share our spiritual journey. We found a warm, supportive adult Sabbath School class at Azure Hills that welcomed this new couple who were in their late fifties. Music collaboration quickly became the best way for me to meet other church members. I joined the church youth orchestra with the intention of mentoring other young cellists. When young people showed up to the events I attended, it sparked joy. I enjoyed spending time with them.

It took an invitation to be part of a reading group with the book *Growing Young* to put me in close proximity and regular contact with generations outside my age group. This reading group opened my eyes to the differing experiences young people could have within the same worship community. I believed that because each generation had their own designated pastor, the youth and collegiate/young adults were well looked after. However, after many conversations, I quickly realized that we could do a lot more.

I asked the young adult pastor, "Is there anything I can do?" She responded, "Yes, we need presence. Just show up." Under conviction, I was led to move from the adult class to the collegiate Sabbath School class to become a sponsor and offer support, empathy, and presence. As a sponsor and advocate, I have been able to bridge the gaps between generations, and now the adult class has become fully committed to pray for me and this ministry opportunity. Coming close to the young adults has helped the group feel visible and cared for rather than being on the fringes and barely belonging. To "feel with" or show empathy, presence is critical.

In the collegiate class, I got to ask simple questions like, "What does your Sabbath School group need?" This conversation led to a growing collaboration between my adult Sabbath School and the collegiate group to provide the young people with food on Sabbath mornings—which has protected our emerging young adult leaders against burnout as they are learning to navigate so much in the new extended adulting process. As *Growing Young* states, "25 feels like the new 15, and 15 often seems like the new 25. Their journey has both an earlier starting line and a later finish line."[11] We must be patient with their maturation instead of assuming that because they are technically adults at eighteen, they know how to run their ministry.

Several months ago, during a group discussion, one collegiate class member shared that he was having difficulty following through on some of his projects. I asked if we could check in on him to ask how he was doing. Since then, he has been making exceptional progress. We would never have had the opportunity to show care and concern without knowing what was important to him.

Think of *empathy* as a verb. Just last week, the collegiate group was asked, "When have you felt scared or unsafe?" When one of the class members answered, "At church," several more nodded in agreement. I am glad that our young adults are feeling safe enough in their Sabbath School environment to say so together. I want them to feel that they belong and fit right here and that their presence makes a difference. We each desire to live in a community that knows the difference between *accountable* and *judgmental*—the difference between being helpful and feeling superior. I do not have all the answers. I do not need all the answers. Every person is so important within our church that we are going to stick with this as a church family. This way of thinking and doing is empathy in action at Azure Hills.

Take Jesus' message seriously
Nick Snell, MDiv, youth pastor, Azure Hills Church

The *Growing Young* authors were struck by how, in the churches studied, "Jesus reigns over poor theology and his words ring true for young sojourners hungry for life-giving direction." One young interviewee said, "The goal for our church is not really effectiveness with young people, but serving and following Jesus. And young people like me are attracted to churches that want to do that."[12]

Naturally a reserved person, she was timid and required support from friends to approach me—the new pastor on staff—to request baptismal studies. I had seen this teen around, but I did not even know her name at this point. Nonetheless, she came and found me after Sabbath School, and though she struggled to make eye contact, she surprised me with her request.

That was not the last surprise I received from Annaliese. As we journeyed together and I listened to her story, I was surprised over and over again at the challenges she had endured in her home, Christian though it was. It was bad enough that she had to experience parents fighting, dad leaving, and a necessary move to live with family members just to maintain a roof over their heads. It was not long before she and her family had to move again because the main provider in that relative's home got cancer just as they were getting their bearings. Annaliese grew up well connected with the church and God, but after going through all that, her view of her heavenly Father was that He was to be hated and blamed rather than loved and trusted. She attributed her trials and losses to Him.

While she, her siblings, and her ever-faithful and prayerful mother were living with her grandparents, they started attending our church. Annaliese felt pained and even jealous as she observed intact families with loving fathers in our congregation. However, over time, these families embraced Annaliese's family, and love crumbled her walls of resistance at the foundation as multiple dads acted as fathers to the fatherless. They spent time together, included them in their family activities, mountain biked together, and listened.

Through the kindness of our members, Annaliese began to hope again, opened her heart to a beautiful picture of God, and began a personal relationship with Him that led to baptism and, beyond that, involvement and leadership in our church. She has gone on to share her testimony in multiple venues, and listeners have been moved to tears by her transformation.

Annaliese inspired her older brother to study and choose Jesus and baptism as well. Not only has she been an inspiration, but Annaliese has also found in this community the support and courage needed to forgive and pray for her dad, even while she has faced the difficult task of setting boundaries with the person she most wished was trustworthy and present in her life.

Taking Jesus' message seriously is not just putting on a nice program for young people and being sweet in every circumstance to minimize disappointment at every turn. It goes way beyond treating others the way you want to be treated. It is wholehearted, passionate, challenging, and lavish grace through sacrificial love that transforms every part of our lives as it surprises us with the truth of who God really is. It does not lower the standard of holiness but lifts Jesus high as the only Savior for all, inviting everyone to take a lifelong journey with Him and one another through the hills of clarity and victory and the valleys of honest doubts and difficulty as hurt is processed and healing is found along the way. We do not just preach; we listen. We come close to the lonely and distressed. We give space to wonder, struggle, and explore—even to do and say the wrong thing and make the wrong choices. However, we are present and accepting through it all. Jesus is the message, and all who join His story are His method as they discover their lifelong purpose and hope in Him for right now as well as the eternal ever after.

I was drawn to Jesus and baptism by a man who took Jesus' message seriously, and I found that fire was contagious. Now, twenty years later, I am motivated by people who do likewise. How about you? What must we as a church be and do? Only pursue Jesus and the places He leads, and the people He brings will surprise you.

Fuel a warm community
Jessie A. López, MDiv, MSW, young adult pastor, Azure Hills Church

> "Warm is the new cool" in these congregations, where authenticity triumphs over worship style or a multitude of programs. Young people who participated in the *Growing Young* research praised their churches for "warm" attributes, such as welcoming, belonging, accepting, hospitable, and caring.[13]

Heart beating. Deep breathing. Feet pacing. Life runs by. Give me a break. We all want a break—a time to unplug and kick our feet up on our coffee table to let loose, be real, and feel at home. In this fast-paced life, people are searching for deep belonging and connection. People are in search of connection everywhere.

Our society craves connection so much that people are even willing to build community with strangers. Social media has created a platform for strangers with common interests to meet and build communities. Strangers make connections through meetup groups, online dating, online gaming communities, Dragon Con, networking conferences, YouTube personalities, group travel tours, and so on. Baby boomers turn to Facebook to connect with old friends to rekindle this sense of belonging. We all live with the desire to share our stories; we want them to be heard. When we do not find belonging, we move on to the next community until we finally find acceptance, honesty, and genuineness. That is when we can tell ourselves, "Yes! This is home!"

Many of our church communities do not offer safe, warm environments that give strangers and young people a sense of welcome. Because of this, it is no secret that the secular society we live in today flinches when they hear the words *I am a Christian*. They see the false and inaccurate representation of Christianity portrayed in media, movies, books, and other sources. Christians are labeled as fake and anti-everything: anti-Muslim, anti-refugee, anti-feminist, anti-black, anti-LGBTQ+, anti-humanity, anti-compassion—the list continues. Unlike other generations, today's youth are fed up with the lack of transparency and are quick to leave religious communities that are unhealthy and unsafe in order to belong elsewhere.

Here at Azure Hills, I am working with the young adult and young professional teams to change this trend of unsafe church environments and create warm and welcoming spaces for all to experience Jesus. Welcoming spaces foster love, belonging, transparency, honesty, and authenticity. This is what young people are in search of: a place that is 100 percent—a place that is *legit real*.

A warm, welcoming space embodies living in the tension with respect for differences in opinions and perspectives. It is a place with no filters. A place where true, authentic language is expressed. A space where people matter most, where belonging trumps belief. It is a community that hears what is shared, affirms what is said, and loves the person who said it, no matter what. As a facilitator for our Sabbath School class and Bible studies, I love to use the phrase, "I hear you, I see you, and I love you." It may sound mushy and too emotional for some, but it has been the core of my ministry at Azure Hills with the young adults. It is real and comes from a place that is genuine. Within the past year alone, our Sabbath School attendance has grown from four to twenty-five. There is no magic trick; it is all in the foundation of expressing that we as a church truly care and love each person—no strings attached.

What does fostering a warm community look like? It will look different for everyone, but for me it includes meeting up with young adults over boba tea or coffee, taking the time to text that young adult back (even though it may be a long paragraph because they prefer to text rather than have a phone call), randomly taking young adults out for lunch or dinner, praying over them alone in my time with God, listening without criticism to their vents over life and religious doctrines, valuing people's differences and embracing the awkward spaces, speaking up for my young adults when people speak negatively about them, and accepting who they are without wanting anything in return.

I have asked my young adults, "Why do you come to Sabbath School? What's in it for you?" Their response is, "Because this is my family." Another said, "I know that we are born into a family, but I love that as you get older, you can choose your family. This is my family. This is why I come." This is what the gospel is about: becoming the family of Christ. Our young adults at Azure Hills feel like they are home!

Authentic and honest relationships build community. This change from program-oriented ministry to personal ministry gets messy and complicated, but I believe it is time for religious leaders to get messy and live beyond the status quo. Our society yearns for warm communities—not unnecessary and insignificant busyness that counterfeits loving religious communities. They want to see their true self. Throw the program out the window and get to know the person who is right beside you.

Our religious communities need people who are willing to be warm—people who are willing to live beyond the status quo, open up, share their story, sit and listen, act with compassion, show love rather than hate, feed the hungry, visit the sick, advocate for the helpless, and lend a hand. Dietrich Bonhoeffer wrote, "The Church is the Church only when it exists for others . . . not dominating, but helping and serving."[14] A warm community serves and exists for others. People do not care how much you know until they know how much you care. Let us open our hearts to the world and let them know how much we love and care by creating a warm community. Let us build a home together!

Prioritizing young people and young families everywhere
D. P. Harris, PhD, elder and church-board leader, Azure Hills Church

Churches in the *Growing Young* study revealed a disproportionate prioritization of young people—an impulse that, rather than excluding older generations, breathed life into the entire congregation. As one pastor put it, "Everyone rises when you focus on young people." Involving young people in every ministry has allowed these churches to thrive with authenticity and intergenerational relationships.[15]

Seriously! It is time to stop saying that young people are the "future" of the church. At Azure Hills, we are committed to ensuring our future by integrating young people into the present. On any given Sabbath, you will see members of all ages serving together as deacons, greeters, or worship leaders. Also, we are learning to create shared experiences in which members of all ages interact.

Azure Hills has active generational ministries as most churches do. Because of our size, we are blessed to have active, vibrant ministries for junior high (eTeens), high school (Powerhouse), collegiate (Gradient), and young professionals (Connect), in addition to various adult Sabbath School and ministry groups. However, through focused energy, we are taking steps to create intergenerational connections between the different groups.

I have had the privilege of serving with the junior high ministry at various churches most of my adult life. Though my boys (ages twenty-eight and twenty-five) are grown, I have served continuously with the Azure Hills junior high ministry since they attended there. Over the years, I have gotten to know a few hundred kids as they passed through. Many have kept in contact well into adulthood. I have contemplated leaving many times, but I find this age so interesting—full of questions and emerging thoughts. They have little patience for platitudes. They are seeking real knowledge, a real relationship with our Savior, and a compelling church experience. And really, isn't that what we all want?

This brings me to the main point. There are a few issues that are relevant only to certain age groups, for example, puberty, dating, young marriage, professional development, retirement. Nevertheless, for the most part, most church members are asking the same questions. The following questions know no age barrier. We start asking these questions in early adolescence, and we never stop.

- Is God real?
- Does God care about me?
- Does God still care about me after what I have done?
- Am I on track to be saved?
- What is my place in God's earthly plan?

So what happens when you bring the generations together? We have tried a couple of experiments at Azure Hills.

Tell a teen your story. For most of 2018, we invited various members of the church into the eTeen Sabbath School. Based on the topic of the week, the guests were asked to share with the class what they thought about the topic when they were twelve. Then they shared how their thinking had changed over the decades since that time. They were admonished not to try to teach or preach—just share. We wanted to give the class an insight into their spiritual journey. The class members were then given a chance to ask questions and dialogue. The stories were as diverse as the Azure Hills multicultural membership. This activity revealed to many members the wonder I have enjoyed interacting with these young people.

Adult Sabbath School excursion. Or should we call it an adult Sabbath School incursion? In 2019, we took this concept to the next level. One Sabbath, we integrated the eTeen Sabbath School with the longest-running adult Sabbath School class. The average age in this adult class was about sixty. We merged the topics from both lessons for the week and discussed, "While we wait for the Lord's return, what role does a Christian have to play?" We broke into small groups, with eTeens and adults sharing together. We gave them two basic rules:

1. Be respectful. Listen well to others.
2. Do not be deferential. Adults and teens should feel free to participate and share as if they were with peers.

It was amazing to watch and see that the different generations could sit in one class and converse as peers on a topic that is of great interest to all of us.

We need to tightly integrate the young people of the church into the entire congregation—not just in service but also in conversations. The youth are pondering the same questions that the adults have been pondering for years. However, unlike most adults, young people are comfortable with their questions and uncertainties and are actively seeking deeper answers.

Be the best neighbors
Sue Smith, BS, elder, Azure Hills Church

The *Growing Young* authors found that in churches growing young, the community accepts the difficult task of offering young people a thoughtful path to neighboring well. They provide opportunities for teens and emerging adults to serve others, pursue social justice, find their calling, interact with popular culture, and respond to heated cultural issues.[16]

In 2017, my husband and I moved to the holy land. Not Israel. Loma Linda, California. For the first time in our lives, we had literally dozens of Seventh-day Adventist churches to choose from. It was our first time as sixty-something empty nesters, and we still wanted to be a vital part of a living body of believers that would appreciate and use our gifts.

Our second Sabbath at Azure Hills, Pastor Tara VinCross suggested "Connect" might be a good fit for Sabbath School, specifically a class called "Gray Matters." The large fellowship hall was filled with several groups of classes—mostly young professionals but also a handful of forties, fifties, and us! I mostly listened that week, but I quickly learned I was welcome as I was introduced to others around the room. The deep spiritual insights and biblical knowledge made me joyful. The atmosphere was open, honest, and nonjudgmental—a place where my husband and I could both give and receive. It has become our home. Good neighbors!

I also found friendships on weekday mornings in the ladies' Bible study, where I was on the other end of the age spectrum. When I am there, I am also among those who love God—but they have a lifetime of experience in church. Good neighbors!

I believe that I should care for my brothers and sisters in the church. I love my intergenerational neighbors! I love delivering a pot of soup if they are at home sick, bringing a box of donuts to celebrate a birthday, or having lunch with them. However, they are not my only neighbors. My neighbors are also those in the community and those in the world.

I am so grateful that Azure Hills facilitates caring for all of my neighbors in so many ways. Our doors are open to over fifteen community organizations weekly. We are truly a congregation that reflects mercy toward the people outside our walls. Some of the ladies make hundreds of blankets for newborns and give them away not only locally but also as far away as India and Kenya. We have a Blessing Bag project for the homeless. We gather new winter coats and make Thanksgiving food baskets for school children in our district. A singing group of mixed ages goes to our neighborhood nursing home monthly. Azure Hills blesses and supports those with missionary hearts to go into all the world, including Indonesia, Papua New Guinea, Mexico, and India. Recently a group from Azure Hills joined our sister church in Tijuana, Mexico, to offer services such as health screenings with nurses and physicians, dental cleanings, and shoe and clothing giveaways.

When I was seven years old, I said to my brother's friend (a boy!) who lived down the street, "I don't have to love you because you're not my neighbor." He wisely replied, "At church, they teach us that everyone is our neighbor." I never forgot that.

I have never wanted to be a spectator at church. I want to tell people how much Jesus loves them, how He died for them, and how He forgives them. But sometimes, before they can hear that good news, they may need to be fed or clothed or just cared for. I love joining with church members of all generations to be the best neighbors we can be—here at home and around the world. This is what unites us.

What if every Adventist congregation were known as a vibrant fellowship where young people thrive and all generations benefit? Growing Young Adventists is on a learning journey where we aspire to make the "what if" into reality. Discover more at GrowingYoungAdventists.com.

Useful Resources

Books

Bonhoeffer, Dietrich, Christian Gremmels, Eberhard Bethge, Renate Bethge, Ilse Tödt, and John W. De Gruchy. *Letters and Papers From Prison*. Dieterich Bonhoeffer Works, vol. 8. Minneapolis, MN: Augsberg Fortress, 2010.

Powell, Kara, Jake Mulder, and Brad Griffin. *Growing Young: 6 Essential Strategies to Help Young People Discover and Love Your Church*. Grand Rapids, MI: Baker Books, 2016.

Online Resources

Azure Hills Church. "Azure Hills Seventh-day Adventist Church." https://azurehills.org/.

Bossert, Bill. Review of *Growing Young: 6 Essential Strategies to Help Young People Discover and Love Your Church*, by Kara Powell, Jake Mulder, and Brad Griffin. *Ministry*, April 2017. https://www.ministrymagazine.org/archive/2017/04/Growing-Young.

Growing Young. https://churchesgrowingyoung.com.

"A Learning Journey to Love Next Generations Well." Growing Young Adventists (blog). http://growingyoungadventists.com.

1. Adapted from North American Division of Seventh-day Adventists, "Growing Young Adventists: Leaders Raise Up Leaders," March 6, 2019, https://growingyoungadventists .com/2019/03/06/leaders-raise-up-leaders/.

2. Adapted from A. Allan Martin, "Growing Young Adventists: Generations Thriving . . . Together," NAD Ministerial, November 15, 2018, https://www.nadministerial.com/stories /2018/11/15/growing-young-adventists-generations-thriving-together.

3. Martin.

4. Bill Bossert, "Growing Young: 6 Essential Strategies to Help Young People Discover and Love Your Church," *Ministry: International Journal for Pastors*, April 2017, https://www .ministrymagazine.org/archive/2017/04/Growing-Young.

5. Bossert.

6. Azure Hills Church, "Azure Hills Seventh-day Adventist Church," accessed October 15, 2019, https://azurehills.org/.

7. Growing Young Adventists, https://growingyoungadventists.com/2019/06/21/brimming-full/.

8. Kara Powell, Jake Mulder, and Brad Griffin, *Growing Young: 6 Essential Strategies to Help Young People Discover and Love Your Church* (Grand Rapids, MI: Baker Books, 2016), 53.

9. Powell, Mulder, and Griffin, 57.

10. Growing Young Adventists, https://growingyoungadventists.com/2019/06/21/brimming-full/.

11. Powell, Mulder, and Griffin, 122, 123.

12. Growing Young Adventists, https://growingyoungadventists.com/2019/06/21/brimming-full/.

13. Growing Young Adventists, https://growingyoungadventists.com/2019/06/21/brimming-full/.

14. Dietrich Bonhoeffer, Christian Gremmels, Eberhard Bethge, Renate Bethge, Ilse Tödt, and John W. De Gruchy, *Letters and Papers From Prison* (Minneapolis, MN: Fortress Press, 2010), 282.

15. Growing Young Adventists, https://growingyoungadventists.com/2019/06/21/brimming-full/.

16. Growing Young Adventists, https://growingyoungadventists.com/2019/06/21/brimming-full/.

A. Allan Martin, PhD, is the teaching pastor of Younger Generation Church—the vibrant young adult ministry of the Arlington Seventh-day Adventist Church in Texas. Dr. Martin serves the North American Division of Seventh-day Adventists as the point person for the Growing Young Adventists initiative in collaboration with Young Adult Life and the Fuller Youth Institute. He worked in partnership with the Barna Group as the lead research facilitator for the Adventist Millennial Study. He also serves as adjunct faculty for the Seventh-day Adventist Theological Seminary, specializing in discipleship and young adult ministry.

Tara J. VinCross, DMin, is the senior pastor of Azure Hills Church in Grand Terrace, California. VinCross was raised in the Seattle, Washington, area and during the last twenty years has served churches in Washington, Pennsylvania, and California. Her doctor of ministry degree is in discipleship and biblical spirituality.

Pastor Jessie A. López, MDiv, MSW, is the young adult pastor of Azure Hills Church. She holds master of divinity and master in social work degrees from Andrews University and has been pastoring for the last seven years. Born and raised in New York City to Puerto Rican parents, culture, family, and food have influenced how Jessie approaches ministry.

DP Harris serves as the vice president and chief information officer for Loma Linda University. He is an elder at the Azure Hills Church, working in youth ministries, and enjoys the active inquisitive nature of young people.

Steve McHan MDiv, is a certified church growth trainer for the Northern California Conference. He served as the collegiate tent director at Redwood Camp Meeting from 2003 to 2013. He is an elder at Azure Hills Church, working with the collegiate and young professionals to put the principles of Growing Young to the test.

Sue Smith is retired from her career in pediatric physical therapy. She is active in the Azure Hills Church as well as mission work, especially for children in India.

Pastor Nicholas Snell is the youth pastor at the Azure Hills Church. Prior to this, he has ministered on school campuses and served both long-established congregations and church plants.

Growing Young Adventists:
How Does Your Church Grow?
Video Presentation (RT: 18:48)
A. Allan Martin

Growing Young Adventists
Video Presentation (RT: 23:58)
Jessie Lopez

CHAPTER 18

Revitalize Churches by Loving Well

Timothy Gillespie

Our journey started on October 25, 2014. I became the pastor of Crosswalk Church in Redlands, California. I learned a few things that first week: (1) Always ask about finances before you take a call. (2) The people who remained at the church after some tough years were deeply committed to both the church surviving and dreaming that it might flourish again one day.

Crosswalk had been a thriving "young adult"[1] group before 2003, when it left the Azure Hills Church to become its own expression of the gospel and Adventist message. Since then, it had soared to about 750 in attendance and had then shrunk to less than 100 attending by 2014. There was a myriad of reasons for the fluctuation, but those are not relevant to this narrative. What is relevant is that there are very few people who are happy when a church is failing.

Whether it is the final few who have stayed, the others who have left, or the conference where the church is housed, no one wants to see a church die. However, we have too often settled for survival as being something we should try to achieve.

Survival is not a mission statement

The best thing about Crosswalk was its mission and vision statement. "Learning to Love Well" created a DNA for the church, at least for those who remained. It meant they were open to new things, new ideas, and new processes. It meant that there was a canvas ready to be painted upon, and this was good news. Congregations need to be one of two things in order to be revitalized: open or desperate. Crosswalk was certainly the former—and very close to being the latter. Some would say this was a perfect storm.

From "Learning to Love Well" to #lovewell

While this mission statement created the right DNA, it needed to be reinterpreted for a new generation, a new expression, and reinvestment into what the church might become. We looked at the mission and decided that for twelve years, the church had been "learning," and it was now time that we executed this mission statement more robustly and palpably. The first step was to drop the "learning to." We decided to take on the hashtag #lovewell as our entire mission and vision statement.

Crosswalk has always had great end statements[2] but seemed to lack the capacity to execute them with alacrity. Rather, focusing on surviving had created a sense of burden for each member. We needed to do something about that. We decided to do a SWOT[3] analysis on the church and all its ministries.

This was painful

It is important to note that this is not an exercise in blame. It does not really matter how a church ended up where it is. What matters is understanding where it is. We cannot move forward if we do not know where we are. All churches should be in a constant state of evaluating their delivery systems. This evaluation is not something you do once a year or once every five years. Rather, it is ongoing with staff, volunteers, the board (leadership team), and the community you seek to serve.

Additionally, a church community needs to understand its economy. This may sound like a strange term to use in conjunction with the church. However, every church has its own economy, or certain things that add value, that the congregation looks for as a sign of success. It is also the thing that creates buy-in, which, of course, increases the capacity of the church to minister.

At Crosswalk, we realized that in a market that is heavily saturated (Loma Linda is the next street over, literally, and the number of churches is overwhelming!), we needed to be different, and we needed to be excellent in whatever we did. We felt this was a distinct and important part of the #lovewell ethos—to always give to God the very best in all that we do. Furthermore, we felt that in order to stand out or find our niche, we needed to understand what was missing in the churches around us and what we could do to fill those gaps. We felt that we could lean into the importance placed on the aesthetic of our built environment, the quality of our worship experience, our desire to engage the local community in ministries of compassion and mercy in a meaningful and sustainable way, and deep study and preaching and teaching of the Word of God.

While these could probably be considered things every church is interested in, we wanted to doggedly go after them with intention and with excellence. We did a few things that led us in the right direction.

1. Constant reiteration of direction in all our messaging. We preached, taught, and made bumper stickers and T-shirts proclaiming the #lovewell mission. Every week, the last word heard from the front was, "Now go and love well." They still hear that every service, every week.

2. Intentional research as to what #lovewell ministries would look like in our specific context. A chapter could be written on how we systematically went about finding the gaps in services our community was suffering and how we could fill those gaps. While not taking all that time, suffice it to say that we surveyed our community with the help of local university students (Azusa Pacific University and Loma Linda University School of Public Health).[4] This process is not fast. It was often frustrating, but it resulted in a sustainable, meaningful, partnerable, and relevant ministry of compassion and mercy to our community. (The short story: We currently have a weekly Community Partner dinner where we serve close to one hundred of the most underserved in our community. This meal is coupled with a weekly free medical clinic and a monthly free legal clinic, which serve the community consistently.)

3. A deep appreciation of the culture or environment we were trying to create. Everything went under review—the lobby experience, the parking experience, the way that the lobby looked, its function and flow, what we offered people when they came into the building, kids ministry check-in experience, technological support in the worship service, the worship experience, announcements, lighting aesthetic, sound experience, and so on. You can see how important every aspect was. The designed experience was reviewed, re-created, and renewed. This process took more than a few months. We had to rework processes; invest in better lighting, sound, computers, and training for our greeters and volunteers; find new curricula for Sabbath Schools; engage graphic designers and space designers; and reenvision what the church can and should be for those God would bring through our doors.

4. Truly become a community of belonging; this is the heart of #lovewell. It is easy for churches to become comfortable for those who currently attend while forgetting about those whom God is preparing to come. We decided to consider the second group first rather than making comfortable those who were already attending and connected. This choice created a desire to help those who came for the first time to belong. Taking the model Belong, Believe, Behave, everyone who came into the church was welcomed as family and friend, brother and sister in Christ. This ethos became the default operating system for the majority of the church. With this in mind, we continued to look for opportunities to bring people into the church through every ministry in which we were engaged. The clinic brought baptisms. The service brought baptisms. Our ministries of discipleship (small groups), preaching, teaching, and compassion brought both people who felt comfortable in the church and those compelled to continue their relationship with Christ through baptism.

Momentum

All of these changes began to increase the rate of change as well as the rate of growth at Crosswalk. Change and growth are great. However, growth can be a recipe for mistakes because what worked with a hundred people will not work with a thousand. This reality means you must constantly make decisions based on the momentum that God gives your church.

Momentum is a Holy Spirit–driven thing. We pray for it, often using terms such as *revival* and *the latter rain*, but when it shows up, you have to be prepared to make decisions you might not have made before, with very little as far as a road map is concerned. Especially in today's world, the tried-and-true ways of building and growing a church no longer seem relevant. That is not to say there is not great wisdom in looking at how things were done in the past, but today's economy of church has been and is changing. It is no longer effective to use a manual to grow the kingdom in today's world.

That means you have to try to create an organization that is nimble enough to change, solid enough to be consistent, and relevant enough to have a voice. Also, in the shifting culture of worship and experience, you have to be able to change on a dime but still stay with the principles the community has agreed upon. When Jesus is your anchor point, the change will not knock you off your course.

Momentum is built by a few things that make a big difference

Four things make a big difference in building momentum: aesthetic, critical mass, mission messaging, and design.

1. Aesthetic. The way the built environment feels helps to create momentum and movement. It also shows your community and visitors that you love well by preparing something special for them. When we made some significant, yet cheap, changes to the lobby in our church, things began to change on a wider level, mostly because people thought things could change. It is somewhat like the theory that says, on a block where something *can* happen, more things *will* happen. It seems overly simplistic, but it builds momentum.

2. Critical mass. Know what the critical mass in your specific room is. Our room fits 700 people, but for some reason, when we get over the 150 mark, the room feels pretty good. This number is not true for every room, but figure out that math in your setting and then work tirelessly to find critical mass. Once you have hit that number, momentum takes over powerfully. The goal is to get the growth to become autocatalytic, or self-fueling.

3. Mission messaging. This aspect cannot be overstated. How are you messaging your mission from the pulpit, through staff and volunteers, through social media and other outlets? Do your graphics speak of mission and have a pleasing aesthetic? Are your greeters versed in the language of the mission that you have chosen? Can they convey, succinctly, the mission of the church? Do you have T-shirts, bumper stickers, and hoodies that all have the same messaging? While you might not think these things matter, are you building a brand that people will pour themselves into? Are you messaging the kind of mission that people can connect to enough to put on a T-shirt or bumper sticker?

4. Design. Design matters; it is as simple as that. How people connect to your community does have something to do with the ethos in which you put the material in front of people. To love well means that you design well. It is the intentional effort that you put into everything that you do that will create the feeling of belonging and a desire to delve more deeply into the community. From bulletins to signage, to the way people move through the lobby, design everything with the end user in mind.

You see, loving well happens when we lose the culture of entitlement and begin to recognize that every person in our church is an opportunity to grow the kingdom and to find another way in which to love well. We should never assume that anyone will come to our church unless it is the place where they can be the most loved and the most cared for, and where they see Jesus with the most clarity. If we are offering something else through our worship, through our fellowship, or through our experience, perhaps we are not on message as representatives of Jesus.

The pain of growth

What you will experience as you begin to make these changes is pain. It is painful because you will lose people who do not like change. To think that everyone will remain happy and comfortable amid such great and significant change is naive. However, you have to stay true to what God is calling you to be. As long as we try to make every single person happy, we will lose our focus, our clarity, and our mission. John 15:1–8 reminds us that a time of pruning is needed in all things that God is trying to grow. The same is true with churches who are changing their focus from volume to value, from traditional to loving well, from stagnancy to revitalization.

You will lose some great and amazing people because they cannot get comfortable with a new direction that your church must take in order to revitalize. These people, as amazing as they are, will be replaced by those who understand the mission, are willing to get their hands dirty to make it happen, and will commit vastly more resources than those who left. Yes, this is a step of faith, but that is what faith is!

Often the problem with churches is that people want things to change as long as they stay the same! That is simply not possible. As management consultant Peter F. Drucker put it, "If you want to do something new, you have to stop doing something old." These words make sense, but they are a difficult reality, especially when the economy of the church has been comfort.

Revitalizing a church by loving well means that you must go through the pain associated with change. Truly, the church must shed the identity most closely associated with those who are already attending and find a new identity associated with those who will be attending in the future. The church has to lean into the idea that God is doing a good work in them, but He is *not* finished yet, and so change, adjustments, course corrections, and clarity are still to come with more power and more moving of the Holy Spirit.

A revitalized church is an expectant church! One that is waiting to see how God will move today and anxious to see where God will move them to tomorrow. Nevertheless, it is also a church that recognizes ministry happens by millimeters, not by miles. While all these changes can be disquieting, it is the accretion of these changes and the power of God that finally creates that momentum and community that we all long to see.

It is beyond our scope to expand the kingdom of God, but it is in His abundance that we work. Too often, we think that there are not enough people to fill our buildings, to cover our expenses, and to receive what we have to offer. However, this could not be further from the truth. A revitalization effort fails when members have a scarcity mentality—the idea that we do not have enough and that God will not bring enough. We are people of faith, and at times, we need to have faith that God will bring the right people, at the right time, for the right reasons. Whether it is money, whether it is time, whether it is the vision, God has enough for every one of us and every one of our communities.

To love well means that we rely on who God is, what God has, and how He is growing and pruning us in order to grow the kingdom through us. These decisions are not easy, they are frightening at times, and they make us feel as though we are stepping into the unknown. However, this is where God does His best work. Rather than staying comfortable and stagnating, I would much rather be uncomfortable and yet see what God is doing every day!

Start with the ending

What kind of church is God calling your church to be? Start with the ending and design backward. Be brutally honest and painfully clear on where you believe God is leading you and your church. Once these things are established, the rest is just logistics on how to get there.

Additionally, trust in God that He will provide what you need most at the right time. All of the growth strategies and church revitalization strategies are worthless without the blessing of the Holy Spirit. Prayer, intention, and belief in abundance will be the guides you need in this endeavor. It will feel as though you are not making progress, but you are—millimeter by millimeter. Eventually, the aggregate accumulation of all that hard work, clarity, blessing, and messaging comes to fruition, and you are now leading the very church you hoped that you and your family could one day attend.

I once spoke to a young pastor who said that he was "hospice" pastoring, just waiting for his churches to die. I was devastated that anyone could look at their ministry with such hopelessness. You see, where Jesus is present, there is *life*! So if Jesus is present in your conversations, in your sermons, in your committees, and in your worship, then your church is heading in the direction of life, not death. For all the tools and strategies, there is only one thing that overcomes the world; His name is Jesus. If you do nothing else, preach Jesus for the next year, and see your church grow! John 12:32 promises that all men will be drawn to Him. Perhaps, we should simply take Him at His word!

---

1. Why is *young adult* in quotation marks? The term *young adult* has become synonymous with a much more relevant and innovative form of worship. We seem to allow for some diversification and variation more easily if they are seen as a demographic other than the main body of the church. This has created many great expressions of the gospel. But it has also created a deep sense of disconnection from the larger church body. What happens when "young adults" aren't so young, yet have no interest in becoming part of the larger church body that is lagging behind the "YA" group in worship expression and relevant ministry?

2. Their end statements are as follows:
    1. Crosswalk will be a community of belonging.
    2. Crosswalk will be a community where people learn and grow in an authentic relationship with God.

3. Crosswalk will be relevant in living out the ways of Jesus in our place and time.

4. Crosswalk will be a community that lives beyond herself by caring and advocating for the powerless, oppressed and abandoned.

5. Crosswalk will be a community that exemplifies servant leadership.

3. For more information on SWOT analysis and how it works in churches, see "Easily Evaluate Your Church With SWOT Analysis Questions," FluidChurch, July 6, 2018, https://fluidccg.com/easily-evaluate-your-church-with-swot-analysis-questions/.

4. An article was developed through this work: Jane Pfeiffer, Hong Li, Maybelline Martez, and Tim Gillespie, "The Role of Religious Behavior in Health Self-Management: A Community-Based Participatory Research Study," *Religions* 9, no. 11 (2018): 357, https://doi.org/10.3390/rel9110357.

Timothy Gillespie, DMin, is the lead pastor of Crosswalk Church in Redlands, California—a multisite church with campuses in Oregon, Tennessee, Massachusetts, California, Colorado, and Georgia. He holds a doctorate in semiotics and future studies from George Fox University and serves as an adjunct professor at both Azusa Pacific University and La Sierra University. He has a faculty appointment with the School of Public Health at Loma Linda University Health. He coauthored a book with his father, Dr. V. Bailey Gillespie, titled *Love Them and They Will Come.*

Crosswalk Church: Revitalizing a Church by Loving Well
Video Presentation (RT: 19:27)
Timothy Gillespie

CHAPTER 19

Accept Transition and Change to Nourish Revitalization

Benjamin Orian

I t was the first Adventist church established in the state of Arkansas (1885) and the second church overall in the city of Springdale. Ellen White spent four days in the city preaching and helping to establish the work here. A few years later, the church opened their first church school. Springdale's population was about five hundred, but within a short time, nearly one hundred people were coming to weekly worship services at the church. With the Springdale church as a base, ten more congregations were soon established, and the Arkansas Conference was formed.

All this growth took place despite serious religious persecution. Arkansas had strict Sunday laws stating that no work, buying, or selling should happen on the "Lord's Day" (Sunday). At least twenty cases are on record of Adventists being arrested for breaking that law. Some of the noted arrests include F. N. Elmore, who was arrested in April 1886 for digging potatoes. James Pool of Fayetteville, Arkansas, was arrested twice for digging potatoes on Sunday. The first time he was fined $30.90 and the second time, $28.40. And Pastor J. W. Scoles was arrested for painting in the original church building on a Sunday. His case went all the way to the State Supreme Court.

Then in 1887, Arkansas State Senator Robert Crockett, grandson of the famous Davey Crockett who fought at the Alamo, stood before the legislature to move an exemption for Adventists who kept the seventh-day Sabbath. The bill passed, and Adventists in Arkansas finally experienced a reprieve from the legal persecution.

Fast-forward to 2018. Springdale is a town of an estimated 81,000 residents. With such a storied beginning, you might expect the church to be a large congregation serving and working in the fast-growing community of

Springdale, Arkansas. Instead, 120 years later, the school is deep in debt and on the verge of closing for lack of students and high teacher turnover. In fact, over the previous five years, the school had to hire new teachers every year and twice had to hire a teacher midyear! What of Springdale Adventist Fellowship (SAF)? It had about 110 people attending, had been without a pastor for more than a year, and was essentially unknown in the community.

Like most churches, SAF has had its ups and downs. Attendance sometimes grew, while at other times, it declined. Pastors came and went. Members were nostalgic for days gone by when Pastor so-and-so did this or that. Nevertheless, most of the active members in the congregation readily acknowledged that something needed to change, and most of the active members willingly voted for change. That is how I came to be invited to serve as the lead pastor at SAF.

In this specific situation, the church revitalization process began in the interview. Up to that point in time, I had been in a great situation. The church I was in was a successful revitalization project that was averaging a baptism every other week with plans of getting to where a baptism happened every week. Attendance was steadily climbing, and our impact in the local community was becoming visible. So when the call came to do it again in a different location, I wanted to interview the church in a way that sent a clear message: I am not a pastor who wants to preside over prayer meetings and programs. I want to be actively seeking the lost, baptizing and discipling new members, and training and equipping those members for leadership and greater ministry impact. So if they were looking for a program and ministry manager, I was not interested.

There is nothing new or insightful about what you just read. I get it. Nevertheless, plateaued and declining churches do not get it. That is why they are where they are. They think that since God never changes, the church should not either. They have fallen into the rut of doing it like they always have, and that is the way they like it. Unfortunately, the longer the church holds on to a tradition, the more sacred it becomes.

There is a certain resistance to change in all of us, which is ironic because change is the one constant in life. Even as a pastor, I fight a constant battle to stay fresh, staying out of ministerial ruts and maintaining a healthy missional focus that adapts to the needs of the community and congregation I serve. My experience in the churches I have served is that everyone is ready for change—until it is time to change.

Is change really the problem? People change jobs. They move across town or to another state. The internet literally changed everything. Social media has changed the way we consume news and information. Almost everyone has a cell phone now. Even a third-grader in the school my daughter attends has an iPhone! It is a changing world out there.

It would be easy to blame the plateau of the church on its inability to change. But what if change is not the problem? William Bridges is an expert on organizational changes who argues that change is inevitable, and as a result, most people do not resist it. He says, "It is not the changes that will do you in; it is the transitions. They are not the same thing. Change is situational. . . . Transition, on the other hand, is psychological; it is a three-phase process that people go through as they internalize and come to terms with the details of the new situation that the change brings about."[1]

The three phases of transition, according to Bridges, are (1) letting go of the old ways; (2) an "in-between time" where "critical psychological realignments and repatterings take place"; and (3) forming a new beginning out of the transition.[2] These phases explain why someone who, today, might not like the changes made in the worship-service order, a year from now, might defend the way it is done. There has been time to transition.

SAF was ready for change, but the transition would be harder than they realized. For a congregation to become a truly vibrant and community-engaged church, it must go through a transitional phase that identifies who they are, what they are doing, and where they ultimately want to end up.

When I arrived, SAF was an evangelistic-minded church with aspirations of planting a church. However, evangelism was largely a series of meetings that, hopefully, ended in baptisms. To their credit, they did have baptisms from their meetings. They would also have ministry events throughout the year, but nothing was really tied to anything else, and no one tracked interests or community engagement. The challenge was to focus the key elements of the congregation's DNA so that every aspect of the church's ministry became both evangelistic and nurturing in nature.

I chose to accomplish this through the three main aspects of SAF's ministries. Those aspects are evangelism, worship services, and community engagement.

Evangelism

When I interviewed the church, I told them that within eight weeks of my arrival, I wanted to begin an evangelistic meeting. Preaching Jesus has a unifying effect on the congregation. While a few may leave, the Holy Spirit engages the interest of most hearers and rekindles enthusiasm for Christ. That spark of spiritual revival is sometimes all that's needed for a church to come to life.

Another reason for an immediate evangelistic meeting is that it shows me not only who is active in the church but also who is potentially going to be active in ministry. Members are still willing to come out and hear the new pastor and will often bring a friend. My first meetings in a new congregation have often been very successful because of this, despite the lack of prework, planning, and visitation that should precede a typical meeting.

Evangelism, of course, is not just about meetings and beasts and prophecy. It is the act of communicating the gospel of Jesus—which means evangelism should always be happening, and every member should be an evangelist! Therefore, revitalizing a church means creating opportunities for members to learn how to do this.

Here is how our cycle at SAF works. Notice the opportunities for members to share with friends, neighbors, and loved ones:

January: We mail Bible-study interest cards. Keep a steady interest in the Bible School.
February–March: We hold a spring evangelistic meeting—usually mid-February to give some of the Bible study interests time to develop.
March: We host a large health fair event for the community.
April: We focus on Easter. It is one of our Big 5 Sabbath events. Attendance is usually considerably higher on that Sabbath, so we go out of our way to make it a big weekend.
May: We focus on mothers. Big 5 event number 2.
June–July: We combine a Fourth of July celebration with Father's Day and do a BBQ picnic out on the church lawn after the service. It is our Big 5 event number 3. Vacation Bible School also happens in July, and we have started putting several thousand dollars into reaching the children of our neighborhoods.
August: The focus is back to school, so we prepare backpacks, school supplies, and other school-related items to distribute to those in need.
September: We host fall evangelistic meetings, inviting all the interests we have met through the year to come for one big event.
October: We celebrate the Reformation at a Harvest Festival. This festival is our Big 5 event number 4.
November: We do Thanksgiving outreach, providing food for families in need. Also, the Pathfinders often are doing their can drives to put food baskets together.
December: Our Big 5 event number 5 is a Christmas breakfast on Sabbath morning, followed by a special Christmas program, usually featur-

ing the kids and youth of the church. The difference with this meal is that I, as the pastor, make it. We do eggs (tofu and real), hash browns, fruit, and veggie sausage links.

Christmas of 2019, I made sixteen dozen cinnamon rolls for the meal as well. I call my rolls "CinnaBens," and I have discovered that this creates a different way for me to engage the members and guests of the church. They expect me to preach and do Bible study, but it is fun, after making the rolls and breakfast, to move between the tables, visiting with the members and guests, laughing in the spirit of the season. In 2019, we had more than seventy guests—most of whom were not Adventists.

The most important reason for evangelism is this: Baptisms. Every month in the calendar, something is going on that helps the members focus on soul winning. Nothing should excite a church member more than witnessing someone being won for Christ. As soon as possible, upon my arrival, I am looking for someone to baptize. When I finish a baptism, I always make an appeal from the baptismal tank, asking if there is another who needs to make a decision for Jesus.

Early in my ministry, I did baptisms when folks were ready. However, what I have learned is that people naturally want to be a part of something. More people than I realized have never made the first decision to follow Jesus, and many more feel a need to renew it for whatever reason. They must be given the opportunity.

Some years ago, I was visiting with a friend who told me he filled his baptismal tank every other month for a baptism. One month, when the tank was full but no one was ready to go in, he went in by himself and asked the congregation who should have been in there with him! I marveled at his tenacity for souls. Right then and there, I asked God for at least one baptism every month. In the first twelve months of that request, I never had to go into the tank alone. Someone was making their decision, and we rejoiced over baptisms every month on the calendar.

Baptism is an essential part of revitalizing a church. Keep it before the congregation. Talk about it. Preach about it. Pray about it.

Worship services

Another key component to church revitalization is the worship time. The majority of your face time with members and guests will happen during your Sabbath School and worship times. Therefore, I maintain that the experience should be so rich and refreshing that people will not want to leave and then cannot wait to get back. Over the years, I have often had members and interests tell me they are rearranging their travel schedules so that they do not miss a particular Sabbath at church.

It is not that every Sabbath is a home-run worship experience. Nevertheless, care is given to the flow, the music we choose, and the sermon and series topics. I preach in series. I want my congregation to be engaged week to week.

Remember this: in a church that is focused on Jesus, soul winning, and creating enthusiasm, and where the pastor or speaker is preaching Jesus, the worship service will be inspiring no matter what happens. Shortly after I arrived at SAF, our regular pianist left. So we had another person who was quite shy step in, though she told us she could only do a few hymns. That Sabbath, the music was slow. I remember standing there as the congregation was singing, just praying that the people who were visiting would understand and not be put off.

The congregation was singing, and there was a sweet spirit in the room. I distinctly remember several guests mentioning how refreshing the atmosphere of worship was. One of the guests, who happened to be a millennial, mentioned how much she enjoyed the music, such a change of pace from her church.

The point is, if it is Spirit-led, Spirit-fed, and Jesus focused—it will be inspiring. Put care and thought into how it is presented. Move things around from time to time. I tell my members all the time, if they do not have to think about what they are doing during the worship hour, then they are not actively worshiping.

Community engagement

I do not know who said it first, but it is a profound question that has probably become a church bumper sticker somewhere: "If your church closed its doors, would the community notice?"

The value of the church must be more than just Sabbath worship, potlucks, prayer meetings, and evangelistic campaigns. A church that is plateaued or dying is usually most worried about taking care of its own spiritual and physical needs. A church that is revitalized and growing is consistently looking beyond its doors to see whom it can care for.

The Seventh-day Adventist Church for too long has been known more for what we believe than for whom we believe in. For that reason, I preach that the church must focus more outward than inward. The fact is, when we focus on reaching others and caring for them like Jesus, all the other problems of the church—the internal disputes, the power mongering, the judgmental attitudes—all seem to disappear. Folks just do not have time to be critical when they are showing Jesus' love to each other.

Let us be known more for the people we feed than the kind of food we serve. Let us be known more for our love for people than our distinct doctrinal beliefs. Jesus said, "By this all will know that you are My disciples, if you have love for one another" (John 13:35, NKJV). If we do that, people will not only take notice of our distinct beliefs but also be more likely to embrace them!

John Knox once prayed, "Lord, give me Scotland, ere I die." Shortly after coming to SAF, we raised the prayer, "Lord give us Springdale, ere we die!" For if the church doors were ever to close, we want Springdale to mourn the loss because of the positive impact and contribution our church will have made to the community.

The results

As of this writing, I have been at SAF for a year and a half. Attendance at the church has increased to between 165 and 180 for most weeks. We now have two worship services: a contemporary service at nine o'clock and a blended service at eleven o'clock. A side result of the early service is that Sabbath School attendance has tripled during this same time.

Our goal in year one was to baptize someone every month. In year two, we wanted to increase the average to a baptism every other week. In year three, we will aim to average a baptism every week. In year one, we met our goal and are on track to meet the goal for year two.

What of Springdale Adventist School? The school that at one time had boasted more than forty kids was struggling to stay open. Deep in debt to the conference and the local church, the school was once again in the process of hiring a new teacher. One of our teachers, whom we wanted to rehire, took a call to another school. The other teacher, who was in her first full year as a teacher, realized that perhaps she was in the wrong role. Unfortunately, as she left, she told parents she would never recommend sending kids to the school. The result was disheartening—all but one parent pulled their kids from our school and sent them elsewhere.

During that year, the school board barely met because they could not get a quorum. Board members would call and say they "didn't feel like coming tonight." Even the lead teacher could not be bothered to come to board meetings. Nevertheless, she then complained that no one was there to help her and no one communicated with her. It was a disastrous situation all around.

In April 2019, the three constituent churches met to discuss whether to keep the school open. Once they voted to keep the school open, I asked the constituent churches to reset the school board. There is no point in having a school if it cannot operate. It was voted that the constituent churches must reelect all members of the school board. Additionally, we established a five-year plan to rebuild school enrollment, the program, and finances.

By the grace of God, we are ahead of schedule. Our enrollment as of this writing is fourteen, which is up two from last year, and we potentially have three more to come at the change of semester. The school has a functional board with good symmetry and a willingness to sacrifice for the school. Best yet, the school will be operated completely in the black this year for the first time in a decade. We have even begun making debt payments! All this, and we are only six months into the five-year plan!

Advice

If I could offer advice to the pastor or laypeople going into a church revitalization project, it would be these six points:

1. Pray! Of course, you know this, but if your prayer life was an hour a day, you had better make it two. Satan loves a plateaued or declining church. He does not need to spend his resources there. However, when a church begins to come to life, it sends shock waves through the demonic world, and he will attack it. He will attack you. So, pray. Pray for discernment. Pray for patience. Moreover, pray for God's victory in your life and the church.

2: Have a thick skin. You understand the devil is going to attack. You should also understand where the attack is going to come from—mostly likely church members. Look, most church members are well-meaning and totally supportive of soul winning, as long as they do not lose or even feel like they are losing their control in the church.

Remember, it is not necessarily the change that members struggle with; it is ultimately the transition through which they must be carefully guided and nurtured. So when the critical judgments and the gossiping take place, understand where it is coming from and respond accordingly. I have discovered that the best response is just to keep your focus on Jesus and preach Him. There may be specific situations and times when addressing the individuals involved is appropriate as well, but do not be distracted by the distractions. That is Satan's plan. Stay focused on the mission. The members will see it in time.

3: Focus on individuals—not the church. People need to feel important and that they are a part of something. Work with a smaller group. Visit with the individuals in that group one on one. Even just a few supportive people can be an encouragement to you, and they will help an unquenchable fire of enthusiasm spread through the congregation.

4: Move from merely being friendly to being loving. There are many friendly churches out there. Walk through their doors, and you will receive a hug and a brochure. Sit down, and a dozen people will greet you. Moreover, you will walk away and say, "Wow, that was a friendly church." However, a loving church cares for its members and its community. When I arrived at SAF, a member who was in the hospital might get a visit. When the invalid came home from the hospital, everything was deemed well. Now, we realize that coming home from the hospital is sometimes just the first step in recovery, and the person has not been home to cook or clean. We are now building teams led by deacons and deaconesses to ensure that those needs are met. By the way, I wrote that last sentence with the present participle, "building," on purpose. Just because you have a team doing something, does not mean you always will. In a revitalization project, you must constantly be working on getting more people involved.

The other part of being more loving was in how we approached community service. One excuse for not engaging is that people are always asking the church for help. Sometimes the people asking are just asking for the next handout. And because so many just want a handout, it can sour the willingness of the congregation to be generous. However, sometimes the need is legitimate. The result was that SAF had a policy of helping up to twenty-five dollars. That will not even fill the average tank with gas today, and sometimes the need is far greater.

We recently reclaimed a backslidden family into the church. Shortly after rejoining the church, she lost her job. Suddenly, the family did not have enough to get by; something was not going to get paid. When they approached me for the church to help, I went to the board and asked them to consider changing the policy. The church did, and now, as long as we have funds, we will pay larger sums of money to help individuals get back on their feet. It really boils down to loving people on purpose and with purpose.

5: "It's not about seating capacity; it's about sending capacity."[3] For a church to truly be healthy, it must be more about ministry involvement than Sabbath morning attendance. When I interviewed SAF, I asked them how many people were actively involved in the church. They told me about twenty-five out of one hundred members. Our goal then, as a board, is to create opportunities for more involvement. Discipleship and soul winning are not about getting people to come to church every week; they are about getting more people involved in soul winning.

6: Just start doing it. I believe God is just waiting to raise His churches to new levels of growth, influence, and community impact. Each church has a unique characteristic and ability to reach others in special and creative ways. Often the church has just forgotten what that looks like, but it will never figure it out until we do something. God has promised us success when we go about His work. So really, the only thing keeping a plateaued and dying church from being revitalized is that church itself.

1. William Bridges, *Managing Transitions: Making the Most of Change* (Boston: Da Capo Press, 2016), 3.

2. Bridges, 5.

3. Rob Paul, "Eight Culture Shifts for Church Revitalization," Rob Paul: Church Revitalization Resources, April 16, 2019, https://robpaul.net/eight-culture-shifts-for-church-revitalization/.

Benjamin Orian is pastor of the oldest Adventist Church in Arkansas. Since arriving in Springdale, Sabbath School attendance has tripled, and a second worship service was started to accommodate growth. Moving churches off a plateau or out of decline has been the focus of his ministry.

Transition, Change, and Revitalization
Video Presentation (RT: 24:34)
Benjamin Orian